CAPITAL CONTROL and the MALAYSIAN ECONOMY

CAPITAL CONTROL and the MALAYSIAN ECONOMY

LAU BAN TIN

Pelanduk
Publications
pelanduk.com

Published by
Pelanduk Publications (M) Sdn Bhd
(Co. No. 113307-W)
12 Jalan SS13/3E
Subang Jaya Industrial Estate
47500 Subang Jaya
Selangor Darul Ehsan, Malaysia.

Address all correspondence to
Pelanduk Publications (M) Sdn Bhd
P.O. Box 8265, 46785 Kelana Jaya
Selangor Darul Ehsan, Malaysia.

Visit our website at *www.pelanduk.com*
e-mail: *mypp@tm.net.my*

Perpustakaan Negara Malaysia   Cataloguing-in-Publication Data

Lau, Ban Tin, Tan Sri Dato'
Capital control and the Malaysian economy /Tan Sri Dato' Lau Ban Tin.
Includes index
Bibliography: p. 161
ISBN 967-978-862-8
1. Capital market—Malaysia. 2. Capital investments—Malaysia.
3. Malaysia—Economic conditions. 4. Malaysia—Economy policy
I. Title.

Printed and bound in Malaysia.

This book is for Charles, Arthur and Elizabeth.

CONTENTS

Preface

The Malaysian economy is export-dependent and has had to contend with the strategic challenges of a rapidly integrating world economy. Government policies have been instituted to address the rapid and high economic growth rates, but these were derailed by the July 1997 financial crisis that impacted Malaysia and the region. Consequent to this crisis, Malaysia's Gross National Product registered negative growth and the massive capital outflow resulted in a sharp depreciation of the Malaysian ringgit.

To cope with the crisis a range of measures was introduced by the Malaysian Government in September 1998. These included selective exchange controls, with the ringgit being pegged to the U.S. dollar at the rate of US$1=RM3.80. There was a one-year holding period for ringgit assets, with offshore trading of the ringgit being prohibited.

While this drew much criticism from the international community, little research has been undertaken on the impact of Malaysia's capital controls on economic performance. The overall objective of this research is therefore to study the impact of Malaysia's capital controls on economic performance. The findings are summarised as follows.

Guided by an analytical framework, this study reviewed the key issues relating to macroeconomic management, exchange rate mechanisms, global capital flows and Malaysia's global competitive advantage. The detailed review and the analysis of the literature permitted the crafting of five research propositions.

The testing, done through a survey and the conduct of focus groups discussions, yielded useful insights on the research problem.

The first of these five propositions is that currency and capital controls are necessary to insulate the Malaysian economy from the shortcomings of the global financial system. These controls have benefited Malaysian firms in that a stable ringgit has helped the economy to cope with the financial crisis. However, the survey revealed that most respondents preferred the capital controls to be removed after 2005, suggesting that the government should critically review the capital control measures.

Next is the proposition that the Malaysian capital and currency controls are innovative and appropriate for pre-empting the problems that could arise from unforeseen massive capital outflow. In arriving at this finding the research also recognised that capital controls could in parallel generate problems, in particular with the country's external reserves.

A third proposition is the impact of Malaysian capital and currency controls on foreign and domestic investments. The research found a sharp decline in foreign investment flow after the imposition of capital controls. There was also erosion of domestic investor confidence.

Fourth is the issue of economic recovery. The findings seemed to imply that there has been a subsequent economic recovery. However, the literature suggested that the recovery could have also stemmed from the resurgence of the global economy in 1999/2000.

Finally, the research findings enabled the formulation of recommendations for consideration by the Malaysian Government in its monetary policies. In the main, it suggests that since the global situation has now changed, and in order to stimulate foreign investor confidence and promote global competitive advantage for Malaysian products, the government should abolish the capital and currency controls. A set of recommendations is also proposed for implementation by the private sector.

The research concludes by identifying areas for subsequent research that should contribute to new theory in development areas.

Almost five years after the 1997/98 financial crisis, many scholars have concluded that the East Asian financial crisis was due to the improper corporate governance and financial system regulation. During these five years, the economic scenario in the west is not much better than what has happened in the South East Asia. The burst of Technology bubble in United States, the wrongdoings of corporate governance – cases like Enron, Worldcom, Xerox and others. All these may sum up to the lost of public confidence. The criticism of cronyism and nepotism in South East Asia from the West is being reflected in the same light from the Western corporate world. In other words, the principle and the practices of corporate governance, which is much influenced by the West need to be revised and reintroduced to the West.

Lau Ban Tin

List of Tables

List of Figures

Abbreviations

ADB	Asian Development Bank
AFTA	Asean Free Trade Area
BIBF	Bangkok International Banking Facilities
BIS	Bank of International Settlement
BNM	Bank Negara Malaysia
CPI	Consumer Price Index
EC	European Commission
EMS	European Monetary System
ERM	Exchange Rate Mechanism
FDI	Foreign Direct Investment
GDP	Gross Domestic Production
GNS	Gross National Savings
IMF	International Monetary Fund
IPI	Industrial Production Index
K-economy	Knowledge economy
KLCI	Kuala Lumpur Composite Index
KLSE	Kuala Lumpur Stock Exchange
MIDA	Malaysian Industrial Development Authority
MIER	Malaysian Institute for Economic Research
MIT	Massachusetts Institute of Technology
MITI	Ministry of International Trade and Industry
NBMC	National Bond Market Committee
NEAC	National Economic Action Committee
NERP	National Economic Recovery Plan
NPL	Non-performing loans
NRB	Non-Baht Account
OECD	Organisation for Economic Co-operation and Development
OPEC	Organisation of Petroleum Exporting Countries
RM	Ringgit Malaysia
SPSS	Statistical Package for Social Science
UK	United Kingdom
USA	United States of America
WTO	World Trade Organisation

Chapter One

Introduction

1.0 Introduction

The Malaysian economy grew at an average of 8% per year over the period 1988-1996. This remarkable performance was aided by proactive policies to promote:

- high growth with low inflation and unemployment
- equitable income distribution, and
- structural transformation of the economy

Bank Negara (The Central Bank) closely monitored the exchange rate for the ringgit in order to fend off periodic attacks by speculators. At the same time it ensured that there was adequate liquidity within the country (*Bank Negara Malaysia* 1999).

In parallel, Government policies were aimed at making Kuala Lumpur a major regional financial centre. Several supportive Acts and institutions were introduced. These included the setting up of the Securities Commission in 1993 and the establishment of

Labuan as an international offshore centre (*Ministry of Finance Economic Report* 1999).

Being a highly open economy Malaysia fell victim to the economic meltdown in July 1997. Following the floatation of the Thai bhat on 2 July 1997, the Malaysian ringgit depreciated from US$2.5 to US$4.88 in January 1998. The stock market composite index, which was at a high of 1,721 points in February 1997, plunged to 477 points in January 1998. The country was landed with a large outstanding private domestic and foreign debt.

To cope with the crisis, the Government introduced a range of measures. These included the introduction of selective exchange controls on 1 September 1998. The ringgit was pegged to the US dollar at the rate of US$1=RM3.80. There was a one-year holding period for ringgit assets with restrictions on taking out ringgit in currency from Malaysia. Offshore trading of the ringgit also ceased, with the currency being legal tender only within Malaysia (*National Economic Action Committee Report* 1998).

These radical measures drew much criticism from the international community. However they appear to have produced some positive results judging from recent economic data which indicate that recovery is underway (*Bank Negara Malaysia* 1999)

1.1 Research Problem

Exchange controls are not new global phenomena. However little research has been conducted on the impact of the controls introduced by the Malaysian Government, and their contribution to economic recovery.

Accordingly, the problem to be studied is "What is the impact of exchange controls for sustainable national economic growth?"

1.2 The Research Objectives and Propositions

To address the Research Problem or the dependent variables requires the identification and address of the underlying research questions or independent variables. For the purpose of this study the research objectives are:

1. To examine whether the currency and capital controls are necessary to insulate the Malaysian economy from the shortcomings of the global financial architecture
2. To determine the extent to which capital and currency controls are innovative and appropriate to address the problems of unfettered global currency flow
3. To determine the extent to which the Malaysian capital and currency controls have contributed to increased foreign and domestic investments
4. To determine how capital and currency controls have assisted in economic recovery in the country, and
5. To determine whether the Malaysian capital and currency controls will enhance the country's global competitive advantage.

Five research propositions have been formulated for testing by this research. These are:

- **Research Proposition 1**
  The currency and capital controls are necessary to insulate the Malaysian economy from the shortcomings of the global financial architecture.

- **RESEARCH PROPOSITION 2**
  The capital and currency controls are innovative and appropriate to address the problems of unfettered global currency flows.
- **RESEARCH PROPOSITION 3**
  The Malaysian capital and currency controls have contributed to increased foreign and domestic investments.
- **RESEARCH PROPOSITION 4**
  The Malaysian capital and currency controls have resulted in economic recovery in the country.
- **RESEARCH PROPOSITION 5**
  The Malaysian capital and currency controls will enhance the country's global competitive advantage.

1.3 BACKGROUND AND JUSTIFICATION

The new millennium is characterised by the emergence of a borderless world (Ohmae 2000). Barriers to trade and financial flow are being dismantled, given the efforts of Governments to liberalise their economies in line with the World Trade Organisation agreements reached at the Singapore meeting in 1995 (*Asian Development Bank* 1997). The tremendous advances in technology, in particular global satellite communications, have eroded the efforts of developing countries seeking continued protection for the financial and trade sectors.

Despite these trends, some countries have successfully introduced and retained currency controls. They include:

- Hong Kong, which relies on currency boards to stabilise her currencies

- China that has a combination of both currency and exchange controls to inoculate the country against the dangers of unfettered global currency trading
- Taiwan which accords special treatment for Qualified Foreign Investors
- India that imposes capital gains tax for foreign institutional investors and
- Chile which has a one-year withholding tax, with 30% to be placed in the Central Bank.

Malaysia is among the top 20 trading nations in the world with external trade amounting to 170% of GDP (*National Economic Action Committee* 1998). As such, she has to take full advantage of the benefits of globalisation, which would increase world trade through the opening up of previously closed economies (Robless 1997). She therefore has to rely on an open trading system to foster investor and trader confidence with a minimum of the controls which impede trade and money flows.

Viewed in this context, the imposition of capital and exchange controls took the international community by surprise. There was much support domestically, premised on the strong belief that the fixed exchange rate and the suspension of capital outflow would protect the country from currency speculators and contribute to economic recovery. However, external commentaries, based largely on "free market thinking", took the contrary view.

Despite the large volume of press reports and commentaries, little research has been done on the workings of the capital controls in Malaysian economy. There is also limited knowledge of the extent to which these controls have contributed to the economic recovery which is underway.

This research is therefore considered timely as the outcome could contribute to the existing body of knowledge and serve as a basis for the formulation of appropriate policy approaches.

1.4 Research Methodology

As there is little literature on the Research Problem it is necessary to have a clearer understanding of the dimensions of the problem through exploratory research. This inductive approach, qualitative in nature, is useful for building new theory and for exploring uncharted theory (Marsick 1990).

The research will:

1. Involve a detailed review of the literature leading to the identification and development of the research questions/ issues and the formulation of the research propositions. This will be followed by secondary data analysis as well as situational analysis to obtain a clearer picture of the situation in Malaysia and
2. Include a primary data analysis, which consists of primary data collected through questionnaires sent to the respondents who are decision-makers of the companies listed on Kuala Lumpur Stock Exchange (KLSE).

On the basis of the literature review, primary data will be collected for the testing of the research propositions. The primary data collection process will rely heavily on the views and perception of Government policy makers. As these policy makers are subject to the Official Secrets Act, sensitive information can be collected only through personal interviews. The data collection is also supplemented by a survey of knowledgeable persons, involving 30-40 industrialists who have been affected by the capital controls. The companies are to be selected based on the overall rating obtained by adding together the individual ratings along four dimensions: the stability of dividend and earnings, financial strength, management strength and future growth of dividend/earnings.

The data collected will be analysed through the use of Statistical Package for Social Science (SPSS).

1.5 Outline of the Research

Guided by Perry (1995) the research has five chapters as outlined in Figure 1.1

1.6 Limitations

The research will be limited to the government and companies being used as case studies. The responses from the selected companies may not be representative.

Secondly, the confidential nature of the industries constrains the collection of sensitive information, especially where it relates to the company's planned strategy.

Thirdly, the analysis is limited to the period from July 1998 to the end of 1999. Due to the changes in the economic structure and world economic outlook, the result of the analysis may have been modified by more recent records.

FIGURE 1.1 OUTLINE OF THE RESEARCH

CHAPTER 1 — INTRODUCTION
CHAPTER 2 — LITERATURE REVIEW Exchange rate systems and exchange rate regimes, global experience of exchange rate systems, capital controls
CHAPTER 3 — RESEARCH METHODOLOGY Data Theory, Exploratory Research, Case Studies, Focus Groups, Survey Sample, Questionnaire, Data Analysis Procedures
CHAPTER 4 — PRIMARY DATA ANALYSIS: THE IMPACT OF THE CONTROLS AND SOME OF ITS CORRELATES Survey background, Impacts of foreign exchange control, Impacts of capital control, Perceptions of ringgit value, Correlations between variables studied
CHAPTER 5 — CONCLUSION Key contribution, Implications for policy and practice, limitations, recommendation on further research
BIBLIOGRAPHY

Source: Developed for the Research

1.7 CONCLUSION

1.7.1 The world currency market has grown to such a proportion that no one speculator or one country nor a combination of countries or speculators can actually influence it. Therefore, blaming a certain speculator or a special hedged fund group for the turbulence in currency market is futile exercise. The currency market grows at the rate of 13% to 14% per year, slowly impeding the government's ability to manipulate, neutralise and control the markets, and causing great frustration among Government officials. Do capital markets then cause loss of controls? Rather than causing loss of control, they shift the power from government to trade corporations, raising questions of sovereignty, accountability and control. However, on closer examination, it looks like the main problem is not lack of control but rather that too much control is preventing *laissez-faire*. Even free western democracies are entangled in government controls and bureaucracy, which impact growth and employment opportunities. Globalisation and capital markets do shift some of the controls from bureaucrats to heads of corporations. But the global market is a function of multiple decisions by multiple consumers in a round-the-clock global opinion. Therefore, it is far more democratic than certain state bureaucracies which never understand how businesses respond and how trade factors function.

1.7.2 Financial markets have changed the relationship between corporations and consumers, as well as that between corporations and the state. While the global market has become both the judge and the jury in some cases, the interaction in general between the state and the global enterprise has evolved into a love-hate relationship. States need multinational corporations to supply capital, create jobs and pay tax. Reciprocally, corporations depend on the state to keep order and provide an educated work force, a modern infrastructure, a stable political situation and a reliable legal system. It is the state forfeiture of some power through deregulation and reduced control that has enabled companies to spread their wings and grow into global corporations. Politics and economics often interact and cross paths in a number of ways. The Malaysian experience for example has shown that many political moves have economic implications and numerous economic strategies have political results. The world in the new millennium has become one global unit, requiring new administrative tools to maintain order and to protect investors. A global central bank for instance, could introduce and enforce uniform accounting standards and supervise national banks, thus providing insurance for deposits, protecting depositors and restoring confidence in the banking systems, as is happening in countries like Indonesia. A global central bank could also coordinate the lowering of interest rates in certain countries to channel capital to others. It could enhance transparency and periodic reporting and take preventive steps in the early stages to halt deterioration into helplessness, as again, in Indonesia. A timely response could direct needy countries to provide a private capital market rather than relying on tax-payers' funds for emergency bailout when it is already too late.

1.7.3 Accepting the authority of a global central bank involves losing control and sovereignty but these are normally surrendered anyway when individuals or groups join a large association. For the present ideology, the benefit of a uniform regulated global banking and financial system would far outweigh the cost of using significant dividend. The benefit includes better-informed and greater investor confidence and the more rational and effective use of capital resources around the world. It is therefore crucial to decide whether Malaysia's adoption of capital control has actually assisted recovery of the Malaysian economy or whether it has in fact merely postponed the greater economic recession to a later date.

1.7.4 The objective of this research is to look into the Malaysian economy and how it has transformed from an agricultural base to manufacturing with a vision of becoming a developed nation by the year 2020. With the onset of the currency crisis, Malaysia adopted the unorthodox measure of imposing capital control, making the

Malaysian ringgit not tradable outside the country. Up to end 1999, the Malaysian government had contended that traditional economic theory does not apply in a globalised world, where the advancement of telecommunications allows information to move at great speed. This research aims to determine whether the selective controls have contributed in salvaging the Malaysian economy or whether they have actually delayed the recession in Malaysia by locking up the funds which had to be retained in Malaysia for one year before they could be taken out. Meanwhile, the economic recovery of Malaysia must be looked at in terms of the impending implementation of WTO and also the economic crisis that is affecting the whole region. Accordingly the overall objective of the research is to formulate recommendations to the Malaysian government on the economic measures required for sustained economic growth within the next five years.

LITERATURE REVIEW

2.1 INTRODUCTION

This chapter offers a brief summary of the literature review on the research issue. Section 2.2 offers definitions and describes the evolution of the exchange rate systems. It also examines the criteria of exchange rate regimes under different systems.

Section 2.3 is devoted to describing the exchange rate systems in East Asia, the UK, the US and the European Union. The chapter focuses on the criteria, differences, and the problems arising from the systems. Besides this, a brief discussion is on the relationship between exchange rates regimes and recovery of the Asian financial crisis as a whole.

Section 2.4 examines the global experiences of exchange controls, which include capital controls and currency controls. In this section, several countries that have previously been involved in exchange controls are quoted and examined.

Section 2.5 and 2.6 focus on the literature review of Malaysia pre-crisis economic weaknesses and Malaysian experience of capital flows. Section 2.7 and 2.8 examine the Malaysian capital and exchange controls and the economic recovery.

Section 2.9 is devoted to identify the research gap, which is possible to be bridged with this research.

Section 2.10 and 2.11 examine the current crisis management of the government, the policies responded to the crisis and the outcomes of the policies, which are reflected in the overall economic performances during this period of time.

2.2 Exchange Rate Systems

The foreign exchange market enables the currency of one nation to be exchanged for the currency of another nation. The market prices of the exchange are indicated by the exchange rates. Thus the exchange rate plays the role of measuring the value of one currency relative to another. (Daniels & VanHoose 1999).

The foreign exchange market, which had already collapsed in the 1930s, was further fragmented after Second World War. In the early post-war years international trade had been separated into a number of groups, which were dominant in different exchange rates, based on both economic and political concerns. (Daniels & VanHoose 1999).

Trade liberalisation in the post-war period has been accompanied by unpredictable changes. The liberalisation could be the result of the actions designed to accommodate new circumstances, some emerged out of crisis and some were the result of avoiding government policies and restrictions. Besides this, the technology has been crucial as it enlarged the scope of operations and reduced the barriers of entry. The evolution in the international trade has not followed any proper guideline. There is no international authority to guide the process. As the globalisation process progresses, the nation state has become less significant. The government's control over money supplies weakened. The investors can now move their capital more freely and production facilities can be located almost anywhere. Eventually, this creates unforeseeable volatility in the market. For instance the crisis which arose in South East Asia. (Daniels & VanHoose 1999).

2.2.1 EXCHANGE RATE REGIMES

All countries are likely to have different and various internal and external policy objectives. The aim for a country to achieve is to obtain internal balance and external balance. Internal balance refers to full employment equilibrium, and external balance refers to a balance-of-payments equilibrium. However, it is difficult to achieve internal and external balance simultaneously. The nature of the potential conflicts between internal and external policy objectives may depend on the exchange rate regime.

There are a number of different exchange rate regimes. The two extreme regimes are firmly fixed rate and freely floating rate. In between the two extremes, there are a number of intermediate regimes, where the rates are partly determined by the market forces, but the government intervenes to influence the rate. (Sloman 1994)

2.2.1.1 FIXED EXCHANGE RATE

Under this regime, the government will undertake any necessary measures to maintain the exchange rate at some stated levels. It is unlikely the internal and external balance can persist for long without the intervention of the government. Maintaining a fixed rate causes changes in money supply. In order not to alter money supply, the central banks or the government has to counter the effect of inflow or outflow of currency through sterilisation.

There are some advantages of fixed exchange rate for a country. With a fixed exchange rate, a country may achieve the aim of maintaining certainty in the exchange rate. International trade and international investment will become less risky. Since the rate is already fixed, there is no room for currency speculators, therefore reducing the cost of government intervention. Other than this, the monetary error can automatically be adjusted. This is because it will force the central bank to support the exchange rate (Sloman 1994).

Fixed exchange rates also produce some bad results. Most importantly, monetary policy is ineffective in this system. If domestic interest rates are pegged to world levels, it is difficult for the government to control inflation since inflation depends on global level. Other than that, the imbalance of current and capital account may persist. The fixed exchange rate regime also violates the free-market-objective. Furthermore, balance of payment deficits and competitive deflation under fixed exchange rate regimes may lead to depression.

For a country in a fixed exchange rate regime (without capital or currency controls) monetary policy will not be so effective. The more a country integrates to the global market, the more closely will domestic interest rates need to be pegged to the world. Fiscal policy is more effective than monetary policy. The greater the mobility of capital, the more the interest rates need to be pegged to the world's rates, therefore, the supply of money changes to reinforce any corresponding result of demand through fiscal policy (Sloman 1994).

2.2.1.2 FREE FLOATING EXCHANGE RATE

Free-floating exchange rate regime is a system where the exchange rate is determined by the demand and supply in the foreign exchange market without government intervention. Balance of payment deficit or surplus can be adjusted through depreciation and appreciation of the currency rate in line with the demand and supply in the foreign exchange market.

There are some advantages of free-floating exchange rate, which are to a large extent the opposite of the fixed exchange rate. Under this regime, the exchange rate is freely floating, balance of payment problems can be solved without the need for specific government policies. Since there is no central bank intervention in the foreign exchange market, there is no need to hold reserves. Besides this, a country is not tied to a high world inflation rate and it is to certain extent protected against world economic shocks. The government can choose any domestic policy as it can now leave the exchange rate movements to take care of the balance of payment effect (Sloman 1994).

Despite the advantages as stated above, there are also a number of disadvantages. The freely floating exchange rate is unstable especially if the demand for imports and exports are highly inelastic. Furthermore, the speculation can be highly destabilising in the short-run which may leave a lot of inconvenience for traders and investors (Sloman 1994).

2.2.1.3 INTERMEDIATE EXCHANGE RATE REGIMES

Between the two extremes of the spectrum of fixed and freely floating exchange rates, there are a number of possible intermediate systems. (Sloman 1994)

ADJUSTABLE PEG SYSTEM

The adjustable peg system is a system towards the fixed end of the spectrum. The exchange rate is fixed or pegged for a period of time, but it can be devalued or revalued at any point of time when fundamental disequilibrium occurs (Sloman 1994).

DIRTY FLOATING SYSTEM

This system is towards the free-floating end of the spectrum. The exchange rate is allowed to float, but the government intervenes when there are violent short-term swings especially arising from currency speculation (Sloman 1994).

CRAWLING PEG SYSTEM

This system is midway between dirty floating systems and adjustable peg system. The parity value and the exchange rate band are allowed to change. The government frequently adjusts the peg by small amounts at regular intervals as the equilibrium changes. (Daniels & VanHoose 1999)

CURRENCY BASKETS

A country may choose to peg its currency to the weighted average value of a basket or selected number of currencies. One of the advantages of choosing this system is that it allows a more stable exchange rate. Under this system, the authority has to pay attention to the exchange rate of the domestic currency and currencies included in the basket and the cross rate between the currencies in the basket (Daniels & VanHoose 1999).

JOINT FLOAT SYSTEM

Under this system, a group of countries have a fixed or adjustable peg system between their own currencies and they jointly float against all other currencies (Sloman 1994).

EXCHANGE RATE BAND SYSTEM

The government adopting the system sets a lower and an upper limit to the exchange rate. It will then allow the exchange rate to fluctuate freely within the limits. It will intervene if the rate hits the floor or the ceiling. Exchange rate band can be incorporated in other systems. For example, crawling peg system with exchange rate band, joint float system with exchange rate band, etc. The exchange rate mechanism of the European Monetary System is an example of a joint float against non-member currencies and an exchange rate band with member currencies (Daniels & VanHoose 1999).

CURRENCY BOARD

Currency board is an independent monetary agency that substitutes for a central bank. Usually the value of the domestic currency is pegged and changes in the foreign reserves in the currency board determine the money stock in the nation. The currency board is thus able to separate monetary policy and the political pressure of the nation (Daniels & VanHoose 1999).

2.2.2 THE GOLD STANDARD, 1816-1933

The Gold Standard system was a fixed commodity system, where the countries fixed their currencies to a physical weight of commodities (Gold). In this system the central bank of a country in this system had the obligation to provide gold in exchange for its banknotes. The volume of paper money in circulation in a country was proportional to the level of reserves. (Sloman 1994)

Britain practised the gold standard system in 1816. Before World War I, Britain was the most important international capital market. Confidence over the strength and stability of the British government and the expertise of the Bank of England made the sterling the foremost reserve currency in the world. Britain left the gold standard in 1914. During 1918 to 1925 Britain adopted a flexible exchange rate system due to the disruption in trade following the war. In 1925 Britain returned to the gold standard. However, returning to the gold standard at pre-war rates and together with the international inflationary pressure and post-war reconstruction, Britain suffered from a large deficit in balance of payment. At this high exchange rate, prices and wages could not be forced downwards rapidly to restore international competitiveness. The situation became even worst when Britain tried to dampen domestic demand by employing high interest rate policy. This led to deepening an already severe depression. (Sloman 1994)

2.2.3 The Bretton Woods System, 1944-1973

After the collapse of the gold standard, the foreign exchange market was chaotic. There were large-scale disequilibria in all the economies. Many countries devalued their currencies in before a beggar-my-neighbour fashion, in order to gain an international competitive edge.

In July 1944, 45 Allied countries met at Bretton Woods in the US to forge a new arrangement. The agreed compromise was the adjustable peg system that lasted until 1971. It was a N-1 exchange rate system, where the US dollar was the pivotal currency. It was also an adjustable peg system. The system allowed for different types of adjustments to address balance of payments disequilibria. The central banks could intervene on the foreign exchange market to prevent short-term exchange rate fluctuations. This enabled them to maintain the pegged rates within a 1% band. For more serious disequilibrium, a country could pursue the policies of deflation or reflation (Sloman 1994).

The International Monetary Fund (IMF) was set up during this period of time for the purpose of providing sufficient funds to the countries, which needed a fund to maintain the pegged rate. Besides this, the IMF also monitored the devaluation and revaluation of the member countries' currency rates.

Over the first 20 years after the agreement of Bretton Woods system, the argument for the system was that it made a significant contribution to the long boom of the 1950s and 1960s. This can be explained by looking at the advantages of a fixed exchange rate regime. However, there were two important weaknesses that eventually led to the system's downfall. The two weaknesses were: the method of adjustment to balance of payments disequilibria and the question of liquidity and the roles of gold and the US dollar (Sloman 1994).

Though the system allowed for exchange rate devaluation and revaluation, in reality it had been difficult to carry out the adjustment. There was the difficulty of identifying whether the deficit (or surplus) was fundamental. The adjustment of rates was also disruptive to firms. Other than this, the J-curve effect might at first make a deficit even worse. This can be explained through the elasticity of demand for imports and exports in the short-run.

Countries with balance of payments surpluses were reluctant to revalue, simply because it would reduce their competitiveness. Deficit countries were reluctant to devalue for political reasons. Since the US dollar was in the pivotal position, even when this country was in deficit, it was not allowed to devalue its currency, because the devaluation would undermine confidence in the system. (Sloman 1994)

After World War II, the US economy was booming, while other European countries were in deep trouble, they were short in dollars. Under the Marshall Plan of the US, European countries were given credits and grants for the sake of financing imports from the US. As a consequence, most of the European countries were seriously in deficit. Due to the lack of US dollars and reserves, many European currencies remained unconvertible. During the 1950s, the US was in deficit, while European countries and Japan were in surpluses. This enabled the countries to move to convertibility. In the 1960s, due to Vietnam War and expansion of multinational corporations, the US was in deficit. The deterioration of the US balance of payment had prompted the US and another nine countries to provide funds for the IMF to support the dollar against speculation. The US tried to curb capital outflows by introducing interest equalisation tax, Regulation Q. However, the outflows of US dollar still continued through other channels. The restrictions in the US also encouraged the development of the Eurodollar market. As the US balance of payments worsened, the US dollar was overvalued. The rate of increase of the US gold reserves did not keep pace with the overseas accumulation of dollars. Consequently, the ratio of the US gold reserves to overseas dollar liabilities deteriorated. Full convertibility of the US dollar became impossible. Following this, market expectation of the US dollar devaluation had driven the holders of dollar to sell the dollar. The speculative attack on the US dollar forced the system down in August 1971. (Sloman 1994)

2.2.4 Floating Exchange Rates, 1973 Onwards

After the breakdown of the Bretton Woods system, the world has been on a floating exchange rate system. Some remain in a pegged but adjustable system, which pegged to a major currency such as the US dollar but floated along with it against other currencies. Some currencies were pegged to each other, but jointly floated with the rest of the world, for example, European Monetary System. Almost all the countries managed their exchange rate. In other words, there was no free-floating exchange rate system but a dirty floating system. Countries like the US and Britain have intervened very little (Sloman 1994).

In the real world, it is not easy to let the exchange rate freely float. This is mainly caused by two important factors. Temporary changes in demand and supply, which can be due to short-term changes in interest rate for the purpose of controlling money supply, can easily cause fluctuations in the freely floating exchange rate. To counteract the speculative movements that may destabilise the exchange rate, the central bank has to act as a stabilising speculator. For longer-term changes such as those due to higher rates of inflation, to a shift in trading patterns or to a change in commodity prices, without intervention, there may be sudden and damaging changes in the exchange rate. The government needs to intervene to allow a gradual and orderly adjustment to the new equilibrium. Besides the economic problems, there are also political reasons for maintaining a stable exchange rate. (Sloman 1994)

There are a lot of problems in managing the exchange rate. One of the problems is that it is not easy to predict the long-term equilibrium exchange rate. Changing inflation rates between countries will require exchange rate adjustments to maintain purchasing power parity. It is therefore difficult for the government to predict the long-term equilibrium level. Due to globalisation and financial liberalisation, money can be shifted from place to place with little restriction. However, this creates a massive capacity for speculation. Besides these factors, the setting of monetary targets and the growth of monetarism have made it more difficult for the government to control the exchange rate. (Sloman1994)

2.3 Global Experience of Exchange Rate Systems

2.3.1 Exchange Rate in East Asia

Before the collapse of the Bretton Woods system in 1970s, most of the East Asian economies were members of the fixed exchange rate system. The collapse of the Bretton Woods system required the East Asian economies to adjust to floating rate regimes.

By the mid-1990s, most of the East Asian economies pegged their currencies against the US dollar. Before sliding into de facto pegging against the US dollar, these countries had been through floating rates and/or changing parities over the period. The exception to the de facto pegging against the US dollar was the Japanese yen, which had floated since the breakdown of the Bretton Woods system. Most of the countries in this region allowed their currencies to float after the set in of the crisis in 1997. The exceptional cases are: Hong Kong and China, which have defended their currencies successfully. Vietnam devalued its currency and fixed its exchange rate. While, Malaysia returned to fixed parity (Samuel & Cheng 2000).

Hong Kong had operated a currency board system, where the fixed exchange rate was supported by the transmission of the deficit or the surplus of the external payments into domestic monetary expansion or contraction. Indonesia had fixed the rupiah against the dollar, but due to high inflation, the rupiah was devalued in 1986. Singapore and Malaysia had pegged against baskets of currencies until the mid-1990s. The Philippines experienced devaluation due to external payment crises. Thailand, Korea and Taiwan maintained a peg against the dollar. However, Korea and Taiwan experimented with a dirty float system in response to payment surpluses in the mid and late 1980s. China mostly pegged against the US dollar or a dollar-dominated basket. The rates were unified in early 1994 at a devalued official rate against the US dollar which has been maintained firmly ever since. (Samuel & Cheng 2000).

The floating exchange rate has been a volatile one. It is believed that a floating rate is not suitable to small economies. Fixed rates can lower the transaction costs and risks for international trade as well as investment. The US dollar has been chosen because most of the capital flows have been dollar-denominated and the US connected; the US dollar is well accepted in international markets.

During the mid-1980s and mid-1990s, most of the East Asian countries experienced growth. Besides the strength of the economic fundamentals, this could be the result of globalisation and financial liberalisation. As the boom continued, foreign investors became more confident in the economic performances of the countries in this region. Thus, more capital was injected into the stock market of these developing economies.

The East Asian developing economies with fixed exchange rates and open capital accounts had not been so effective in adjusting the imbalance caused by the boom. Monetary policies cannot be effective under a fixed exchange rate regime. Employing tightening monetary policy could not solve the inflationary pressure arising from the inflows of capital. This was simply because when the government raised its interest rate to ease the inflationary pressure, foreign funds would be attracted to the high interest rate, offsetting the monetary tightening.

The US dollar was not suitable as an exchange rate peg especially when the dollar was appreciating against most currencies. The peg had led to a real appreciation after 1995. Since the established exchange rate systems were not suitable for the East Asian developing countries, other exchange rate systems such as freely floating rates or rate fixed within a currency board needed to be considered.

For a freely floating regime, a booming economy with strong capital inflow and external payment surpluses, currencies would appreciate. This would then reduce the boom and inflationary pressure. It is inevitable that later downward reassessments of East Asian investment opportunities would have led to smaller and real depreciations. The earlier real exchange rate could cut off some opportunities for growth. The extent of depreciation would be hard to be determined, since floating rates typically overshoot in adjustment to new circumstances or a new equilibrium. (Samuel & Cheng 2000).

An economy with rigidly fixed exchange rates within a currency board system in the year before the crisis may have led temporarily to an exacerbation of real exchange rate appreciation. This would increase the costs of the boom and could probably have brought the boom to an early end. Therefore, the economic shock would not be so large and sudden. Though it cannot be stated that the exchange rate regimes in place in the mid-1990s were the cause of the recent financial crisis, the evidence points to the exchange rate regimes playing an important part in the depth and extent of the crisis. (Samuel & Cheng 2000).

2.3.2 Exchange Rate in the UK and the US

The 1973/74 oil crisis had given a shock to the world economy. Countries could not depreciate their exchange rate because it would cause a further rise in inflation and little increase in exports. The increased oil price led to both inflation and recession. In order to solve this problem, the UK had to attract surpluses from OPEC, and it undertook large-scale foreign borrowing. Together with this, the UK also used reserves to maintain a stable exchange rate. This policy was successful, but from 1975 onwards, the exchange rate began falling. The falling exchange rate gathered momentum and it became even worse when speculation set in. Short-term deposits were withdrawn from the country and these forced the country to negotiate a loan with IMF. The exchange rate bottomed out at the end of 1976 after implementing deflationary measures were introduced.

The measures taken by the UK and the North Sea oil had helped to restore confidence in sterling. The government continued to intervene in the foreign exchange market until 1977, and then the sterling was allowed to float. Up to 1981, the pound sterling had appreciated by about 30%. The appreciation decreased international competitiveness and imports to the country became so cheap that they drove out local firms. This contributed to the recession. (Sloman 1994)

During 1981-1985 the US hoped to maintain a balanced budget by adopting to so-called "Reaganomics". Increases in defence expenditure and government expenditure had led to a growing budget deficit. Given the commitment to monetarism, the deficit had to be financed by borrowing, and this in turn led to a higher interest rate. The high interest rates attracted foreign capital into the US and thus created a surplus in the capital account. Increasing aggregate demand led to a current account deficit. The capital inflow caused the appreciation of the US dollar. In other words, the US had a current account deficit and at the same time, an appreciating the US dollar. In order to maintain a high US dollar while the current account deficit increased, the US continued its high interest rate policy.

OPEC deposits in the UK were channelled to the US due to the high interest rate compared to the UK. The capital flight had caused a crisis in the UK in 1985. Large amounts of dollar reserves and other reserves had been sold, interest rates were raised and a minimum interest rate was introduced. However, the crisis would only solved when there was a concerted action between European central banks and the Bank of Japan. After this the destabilising speculation had worked to drive the US dollar down.

The US dollar had not returned to its high levels for a long time. Sterling at first appreciated. As a petrocurrency, it depreciated when oil prices fell. Sterling began to rise again in 1987. To maintain the exchange rate, the pound sterling was then pegged to the German mark. (Sloman 1994)

The UK's deficit in its current account during late 80s, had given rise to panic selling of sterling and to capital outflows. The Bank of England frequently had to intervene in the foreign exchange market. The weakness of the pound sterling and the rising inflationary pressure forced the UK government to join the Exchange Rate Mechanism aligned with other EC countries. (Sloman 1994)

2.3.3 Exchange Rate and EMS

In 1978, it was agreed that a European Monetary System be established. The aim of the EMS was to create currency stability, monetary cooperation and the convergence of economic policies of the EC countries. One of the most important features of EMS was the Exchange Rate Mechanism (ERM). ERM was a parity grid system where a currency was denominated in terms of the other ERM currencies in a grid. A currency within the system was pegged with other ERM currencies and fluctuation was only allowed within a specified limit. The parities were adjustable and all the currencies within the system float together with currencies outside the ERM.

The advantages of ERM were that trade will be encouraged within the member states, more harmonisation policies to be employed within member countries. The combined reserves of the bloc countries can be used to prevent fluctuations of the bloc's currencies with others.

There were some rules to limit the fluctuations of each member currency (Sloman 1994 and Williamson & Miller 1987). First, each currency was allowed to fluctuate to a certain percentage either side of each other currency. The system was known as the snake in the tunnel. If a currency reached the upper or lower limits against any other ERM currency, the two countries must intervene so as to maintain their rates within the band. Second, each country had a central parity against the ECU (European Currency Unit). Though it was first seen to be optimistic, the system ceased to operate in 1992/93 (*European Economy Annual Report* 1993).

Some argue that the collapse of the system was due to the underlying weaknesses of the system. The establishment of ERM had effectively removed capital controls (Shirreff 1993) and made the ERM currencies vulnerable to speculative attack. The UK had joined the system with a high rate, forcing the UK to keep its interest rate high to protect its currency. The reunification process of Germany caused budget deficit and French franc was perceived to be too high.

After the breakdown of ERM, the Maastricht Treaty set out the path towards a single economy for the EC countries. It set out a programme for economic and monetary union (EMU). In January 1999, a single European currency (EURO) was created. The single currency has eliminated the costs of converting currencies. It also removes the problems of uncertainty about exchange rates. Furthermore, countries can employ a single monetary policy.

2.3.4 Exchange Rates Regimes and Recovery

Exchange rate regimes play an important part in economic recovery. Some changes in economic conditions are needed for the recovery. They are increasing domestic demand, International competitiveness, restoration of balance in external payments, stronger banking and financial assets and real business opportunities.

It seems that during a crisis, the economies with firmly fixed rates can maintain confidence in domestic financial assets, and reduce the pressure on domestic banks and financial institutions. On the other hand, economies with adjustable rates, such as Thailand, Korea and Indonesia in the crisis of 1997, are required to devalue the assets of domestic financial institutions to an extent beyond those institutions' capacity to manage.

It has not been easy to make comparisons of exchange rate regimes. The government attempts to hold up interest rates by raising interest rates. However, this may not attract capital inflows because at the same time, they are associated with recession and diminished confidence.

One of the advantages of floating exchange rate over fixed exchange rate is that it provides the freedom to set monetary policy to meet the requirements of the domestic economy. The floating exchange rate also improves competitiveness of an economy more quickly than the firmly pegged rate. Hence there are rapid increases in net exports. However, the weakened banking systems and decreasing demand can hold back export expansion, the descent into recession can be greater and faster than anticipated early in the crisis.

2.4 EXCHANGE CONTROLS

Exchange controls are normally used to overcome balance of payments problems. The paradigm of a comprehensive system of exchange controls would have certain characteristics: First, residents would not be permitted to transfer the state's currency to non-residents except with permission. Second, non-resident holders of the state currency would not be allowed to transfer their holdings to residents except with permission. Third, the residents would not be permitted to hold foreign currencies without the state's permission. (*IMF* 1983)

Countries with comprehensive exchange controls would usually enact laws so that the authorities can implement the control policy. The controls may vary in the degree of restrictiveness.

2.4.1 Currency Controls

2.4.1.1 Controls on the Holding, Use and Transfer of the Issuing – State's Currency

Countries that impose such a control may fear that if its residents were allowed to transfer the domestic currency to foreigners in payment for all kinds of international transactions, the result would be increased imports, capital flight and currency depreciation. Some countries require non-residents to open an account with a local bank; there could be different rules on the permitted use of funds. The governments usually have the rights to control any international transactions involving the exchange of local currency with foreign currencies.

2.4.1.2 Controls on the Holding, Use and Transfer of Foreign Currencies

Governments can impose controls for the purpose of centralising foreign-currency holdings for use in the country's policies and plans. The exporters are required to register their exports. The government can determine which are the designated currencies to be accepted in international transactions. The residents, under such a control regime, are also required to obtain that currency from, and to sell any acquired foreign exchange to, the governmental agency or authorised banks when they want to make payments and receive payments[1]. This is a common feature of currency control systems, which is called a surrender requirement. Some countries with surrender requirement sometimes also establish retention quotas. With this quota exporters from the state are allowed to keep and not surrender a portion of the foreign currencies received. The reasons for establishing retention quotas are: to avoid administrative costs associated with collecting exchange, to act as an incentive to exporters to demand payment in one of the quota currencies. For example, in some countries with retention quotas, the exporters are allowed to retain a part of the currencies received and may be able to sell it in the private market at premium price[2]. (IMF 1983)

2.4.1.3 MULTIPLE EXCHANGE RATES

Different exchange rates for different classes of transactions can be imposed on the international transactions of a country. These act as taxes and subsidies upon trade. According to research, this policy distorts economies and is difficult to administer. Further, it raises the cost of currency for any class of current transactions and does not promote a stable system of exchange rates. Countries that practice multiple exchange rates include Argentina, the Dominican Republic and Mexico. In some economies for example, exchange for current transactions takes

---

[1] The monetary board in Colombia, in order to prevent Colombian exporters from unlawful declaring and surrendering substantial less foreign exchange than they receive, sets minimum surrender prices for coffee, bananas and other products. The exporters are required to surrender proceeds in a quantity not less than the minimum surrender price. If the minimum export prices are unrealistically high, they can inhibit export.

[2] Pakistan's export-bonus-voucher scheme for sales of non-traditional item in 1959-72 is illustrative.

place at one rate and exchange for capital transactions take place at a different rate. During September to December 1982, Mexico practiced this two-tier exchange system with two different official rates.

2.4.1.4 Discriminatory Currency Arrangements

Discriminatory currency arrangements can take a variety of forms. The most important are Bilateral Payments Agreements. Countries that are parties to bilateral agreements encourage importers and exporters to buy from or sell to bilateral partners rather than the international market. Mexico, Ecuador, Finland, The People's Republic of China, Costa Rica and Peru are some of the countries, which used to have such an arrangement[3]. (*IMF* 1983)

2.4.1.5 Limitations on Travel Allowances

Currency restrictions can be imposed on travel allowances. This aims at not just controlling expenditures but also controlling capital movements. Many countries used to impose such a restriction although normally the restriction is temporary. For example, Argentina, Costa Rica, Dominican Republic, El Salvador, Guyana, Guatemala, Jamaica, Mexico, the Netherlands, Peru and recently, Malaysia.

2.4.2 Controls on Capital Movements

Capital movements are the monetary movements associated with both direct and portfolio investments, loans, insurance and others. They are not related to trade. Controls on outward

---

[3] As of 31 December 1982, there were 62 operative bilateral payment agreements between pairs of IMF members.

monetary movements may be used to assure that capital is not flowing outside the country. They also restrict the transferring of domestic currency or savings out of the country and the repatriation of proceeds by non-residents investors upon the liquidation or sale of local direct investment, especially when the country is facing problems such as, decline in purchasing power or political instability.

The authority may use this strategy to utilise the country's resources. Controls also enable the country to avoid the cost of defending its currency and to adjust the balance of payments. Direct investments abroad by residents often need the approval from the government. Besides these, it can be other restrictions such as the control of gifts made to non-residents abroad and control on the purchase of investment products from other countries. (*IMF* 1983, pp.252. *OECD*, 1980)

For example, The United States at one time imposed an interest equalisation tax on purchases by residents of stocks, bonds, and other investment securities issued abroad when the purchase was made from foreign investors.

There are also measures to prevent circumvention of capital controls include requiring approval of monetary authorities for a resident to hold currency balances abroad, placing limitations on the size and the usage on the approved holdings, limitation on the business and tourists' travelling expenditures. For the transportation of currency, stock, bond certificates, gold, jewellery and other investments may required to obtain prior approval.

There are different motivations behind the restrictions or the controls on the entry of foreign capital into the country. Many countries use some techniques such as investment screening to bar investment by non-residents. For example, Canada reviews the foreign investment proposals and takes balance of payment into consideration. Some countries may restrict residents from investing in foreign companies. There are countries which bar investment in most businesses and industries, for example Romania (central-planned country).

Globalisation and financial liberalisation has changed the world, which is becoming more integrated. Short-term flows of capital are encouraged when there are differentials in international interest rates and exchange rates. Capital flows are mainly from industrial countries to developing countries. A country may use the techniques described above to cope with disturbing in- or out-flows of capital. However, it is not always easy to distinguish whether they are short-term or long-term. (*IMF* 1983)

To prevent the effect of overheating short-term capital transactions, the authorities can use a variety of monetary instruments, as well as other official measures. (Mills 1996 and *OECD* 1982)

2.4.3 GLOBAL EXPERIENCES OF CAPITAL CONTROLS

Malaysian's decision on capital and currency controls in 1998 created a shock to the world. However, such controls are not new to the world. Some countries have started practicing capital controls as a means to reduce exchange rate fluctuations in the past. Some examples of developing countries that have used capital controls strategy are Chile, Brazil, Colombia, Czech Republic, Thailand as well as ERM countries. (*IMF* 1983)

2.4.3.1 CHILE

The growing capital inflows to Chile in 1990 prompted the central bank to undertake intervention to curtail exchange rate appreciation and contain monetary expansion. However, this strategy raised domestic interest rates and attracted short-term capital inflows.

In order to curb the overheating created by capital inflows, the Chilean government decided to impose controls on short-term inflows. Chile has three types of controls. First, a 30% of reserves requirement to be deposited in central bank without interest. this acts as a tax to capital inflows; the effective tax rate becomes very high for short-term capital inflows. Second, foreign investment in Chile must exceed US$1 million and the foreign money has to stay in the country for more than one year. Third, if any domestic firm wants to tap funds from the international market, the firm must obtain two bond-rating agencies to rate their bonds or any financial instrument as high as Chilean government bonds. On some occasions, the Chilean government has encouraged capital outflows, for example, the relaxing of restrictions on pension fund investment. Capital control in Chile is successful in terms of being able to reduce inflows of short-term foreign money since 1991. (Maxfield 1998)

2.4.3.2 BRAZIL

In mid-1994, Brazil experienced a severe inflation of around 2,200% per annum. The imposed monetary policy and measures, together with exchange rate stability, had attracted capital inflows. In view of the fear that inflows of foreign money could increase private consumption, the government put into practice some controls. First, it raised taxes on bonds issued abroad by domestic firms from 3% to 7%. Second, it levied a 1% tax on foreign investment in the Brazilian stock market. Third, it increased tax on foreign purchase of domestic fixed-income investments from 5% to 9%. Despite all the taxes imposed, inflow of foreign money still continued. This implies that small tax increases do not have much effect on the volume of capital inflows.

2.4.3.3 COLOMBIA

Similar to other countries in Latin America, Colombia experienced massive capital inflows during the 1990s. The central bank in Colombia implemented sterilised intervention to alleviate currency appreciation. The central bank foreign exchange issued local bills to absorb injected liquidity. However, the cost of the intervention was too high because the interest paid on the domestic bills exceeded those earned on additional foreign reserves. The government then decided to allow the rate to go up. By 1993, due to the discovery of oil, Colombia attracted capital inflows. The government had no choice but to impose controls such as those imposed by Chilean government.

2.4.3.4 CZECH REPUBLIC

The appreciation of Czech koruna and the differentials of the domestic and international interest rates had attracted abundant capital inflows to the Czech Republic. The government's reaction to this was to impose sterilised intervention and then a 0.25% tax on foreign exchange transactions with banks. Later, banks' short-term foreign borrowings were limited to 30% of claims on non-residents or 500 million koruna, while, non-bank lenders need to seek advice or approval from the government before borrowing from abroad.

2.4.3.5 THAILAND

Thailand's strong economic fundamentals and stable exchange rate attracted a stream of capital inflows. However, the inflows were mainly short-term. These were mainly channelled through Bangkok International Banking Facilities (BIBF) and non-resident baht accounts (NRB). By 1995, a liquidity requirement of 7% on short-term NRB was imposed. The out-in BIBF also rose from US$500,000 to US$2 million. In the mid-1996, a 7% requirement for non-remunerated deposits at the central bank was introduced, applicable to commercial banks and finance companies. However, the imposed measures were not successful.

Besides these countries, Argentina, Hong Kong, China, Taiwan and India have also utilised retaining currency and capital controls. Hong Kong and Argentina rely on currency boards to stabilise their currencies. China has a combination of currency and exchange controls to avoid currency speculation and unfitted currency trading. Taiwan employs discriminative treatment for qualified foreign investors only. India imposed a special capital gain tax on foreign investment. (*IMF* 1983)

Capital liberalisation is basically good to a developing economy. It allows the emerging countries to import capital, technology and hence innovation. Provided with a sound financial system, a country can grow faster with it. However, according to Roberto Zahler, former governor of the Central Bank of Chile, the real interest rates in developing economies are higher than those in developed countries. This implies that the investment in developing countries can earn higher returns.

When massive capital pours into a developing economy, the interest rate should gradually decline to the level of developed countries. This can only be achieved if there is rapid and severe inflation. Thus it may lead to a bubble economy (*The Economist* 1998).

Further, it may lead to a current-account deficit, especially to a small country. Therefore, currency controls or capital controls do help stabilise an economy, as well helping to avoid unwanted crisis or bubble economy (Maxfield 1998).

2.5 Malaysian Capital and Exchange Controls

According to Mead (1998), the Asian currency crisis caused considerable soul-searching among some quarters about the much-trumpeted superiority of export-oriented industrialisation as a development strategy. After all, it was the export-oriented economies that were hardest hit. What had been touted as the preferred path to rapid economic growth and development had instead led to economic ruin in Asian countries (Mead 1998).

Studies done by the World Bank (1998) had suggested that the crisis was the result of poor domestic policy. The current account deficit and economic bubble were the result of the overheating economies. Together with inadequate supervision and management in financial systems, banks and corporations borrowed large amounts of money from the international capital market, much of it being short-term. Inflowing foreign funds were put into poor-quality investments. The governors were not providing accurate and sufficient information. A lack of transparency and accountability had given rise to the problem of adjustability of the policy (both private and public sectors). Furthermore, inappropriate financial liberalisation and poor regulatory systems encouraged excessive risk-taking. When the crisis broke out, the value of external debts increased in terms of domestic currency, creating a solvency problem. As debts mounted, firms had to obtain more dollars to close up open positions, hence leading to the depreciation of exchange rates (*World Bank* 1998).

Besides the IMF and the World Bank, Professor Paul Krugman (1998) of the Massachusetts Institute of Technology pointed out that the crisis was due to macroeconomic policy slippages and weaknesses in the financial systems. Unregulated banking institutions encouraged moral hazards, leading then to unrealistic speculation, imprudent lending practice and inefficient allocation of resources. The payments disequilibria and weak economic fundamentals led to the currency and equity markets meltdown (Krugman 1998).

In order to solve the crisis problems, capital controls were introduced in Malaysia. In fact, the September 1998 capital controls were not new to Malaysia and other parts of the world. Temporary capital controls had been introduced in early 1994 after an experience of massive capital flight with the sudden reversal of massive net portfolio capital inflow in 1992-93 (Jomo 2001).

The imposition of capital controls with a fixed exchange rate for the Malaysian ringgit allowed the Malaysian government to follow expansionary fiscal and monetary policies, which was the policy reversal taken by the government after March-August 1998.

Critics have pointed out that the capital controls are a time-buying device for reforming the financial and industrial sectors rather than for bailing out unviable companies. In other words, the control is useful only if the government maintains tight controls on political freedom, while allowing the market to function relatively freely (Bhanoji Rao 2001).

Other arguments against the Malaysian capital controls include the opinion that the recovery would have come any way due to the resumption of capital flows to the region, the recovery of regional economies and the strong US economic growth (Lim 1999).

The Malaysian recovery does not indicate whether the economy has benefited relatively more from capital control than if the government had gone to the IMF. The positive side of the capital control is the fact that it has not added the burden of extra external debt, which would have been perhaps of the order of at least some US$20 billion if an IMF programme was sought. The minus side is that domestic economic agents are sheltered by the fixed exchange rate (Bhanoji Rao 2001).

In his research, Jomo K.S. (2001) concluded that capital controls have not caused the recovery in Malaysia to be slower than it had in the other countries facing the same crisis. Though the recovery in the Malaysia economy has been faster since early 1999, Malaysia missed out on most of the renewed capital flow into the region from the final quarter of 1998. To him, the most critical challenge ahead is the credibility of future government policies.

The pegged ringgit has not really boosted the export sector of the country. As the export base remains narrow and comprising mainly of manufactured goods such as electronics and electrical goods, the increase in the foreign reserves situation has resulted largely from massive import compression. There are costs to maintaining an undervalued ringgit. Although the undervalued ringgit may help some exports in the short-term, it also makes imports of capital and intermediate goods more expensive, thus impeding economic recovery and capacity expansion in the medium term (Jomo 2001).

The controls have also had negative effects on the economy. The Malaysian government's policy of consistency and credibility has been seriously undermined. As Jomo suggested, the current regime is counter-productive and will have adverse consequences if it is the intention of the government to retain the regime until such time as the international financial system is reformed. The government should institute a permanent but flexible, market-based regime of prudent controls to moderate capital inflow and deter speculative surges, both domestic and foreign, to avert future crises (Jomo 2001).

There are also arguments suggesting that financial governance is important, and that good policy design in itself cannot guarantee good outcomes. Good policy can fail because of poor implementation or enforcement and the lack of political will. The 1997/98 financial crisis seems to suggest that Malaysia's economic boom in the 1990s had been built on vulnerable and unsustainable foundations. Much of the wealth retained was then re-invested to capture rents in the protected domestic economy. Crony-rentierism has been condemned as the source of the economic debacle (Jomo K.S. & Hamilton-Hant 2001).

2.6 Capital Flow: The Malaysian Experience

2.6.1 Capital Flow

Many Southeast Asian countries have recently undertaken both financial liberalisation and capital account liberalisation. The process had in fact started in the 1970s, with the first round of liberalisation being the liberalisation of the financial markets. Banks became more competitive and were able to offer a range of products including off-balance-sheet products and to create quasi-banking operations. Furthermore, domestic firms became less reliant on finance from banking institutions and started moving toward market-oriented finance. At the same time, barriers of entry have been removed. As foreign banks were allowed to have a larger stake in the financial sector, more banks were set up in this region (Ross 1998).

The liberalisation of the capital account also relaxed the restrictions on non-residents' capital accounts that in turn encouraged more capital inflow into the region. Consequent to this inflow of foreign funds, domestic firms became heavily dependent on external finance. Countries welcomed the inflow of the funds because they were capital-short. The inflow provided additional capital, which helped to avert the problems of distribution between gainers and losers. New entrants could compete with established rivals. The international interest rate was basically lower than the domestic interest rate. It encouraged foreign borrowing and permitted the flourishing of offshore banking operations. Furthermore, the opening of the capital account also enabled access to the markets by foreign fund managers (Kwan 1998).

Financial liberalisation brought capital inflow into East Asian countries. Capital from abroad provided important sources of funds for building infrastructure and developing human resources. However, capital inflow also distorted relative prices and fed asset-price bubbles. According to the established method of analysing financial liberalisation, the Southeast Asian countries had done very well. However, the liberalisation had at the same time unconsciously created the conditions for a banking crisis in these countries. It gave rise to a property bubble, which led to a boom in private lending, resulting in a dramatic increase in non-performing loans. Indonesia and Thailand were the most affected by this problem during the crisis. Indonesia was already experiencing banking failure even before the onset of the crisis. In comparison, Malaysia, the Philippines and Singapore had more effective and prudent supervision over their financial systems (Montes 1996).

The liberalisation of capital account and inflow of foreign funds to Asian countries helped the countries in this region to achieve high growth. However, recent crises such as the Mexican one in 1994 and the Asian currency crisis in 1997/98 remind us of the possible reverse effect of massive inflow of short-term funds.

There are a number of factors that accelerate the liberalisation of capital accounts in these countries. One of them is the global trend toward financial liberalisation and globalisation or internationalisation of money and capital markets. Secondly, many developing countries have responded to external pressure to open their capital markets and remove exchange controls. It has also become a prerequisite for countries to liberalise their capital accounts in order to join international organisations such as OECD and WTO (Kwan 1998).

Some critics have pointed out that the Asian capital market crisis reflected the degree of exposure of Asian countries to external financial instruments, which had rendered the economies vulnerable to various developments. The vulnerabilities arose because of the mismatch of assets and liabilities in terms of maturities and currency denominations. Besides this, external funds were raised to purchase foreign financial products. All these factors contributed to a fragile financial system. Other external factors adversely affecting the trade environment in East Asia included the Japanese economic slow-down and the sharp fluctuation of the yen against the US dollar. These factors increased the vulnerability of Asian countries (Dornbusch, Rudiger, Iian Goldfajn & Rodrigo 1995).

Professor Jeffrey Sachs of Harvard University pointed out that the countries affected in this round of crisis were in fact fundamentally sound. The problems arose from the rapid liberalisation in international markets. There was inadequate preparation for dealing with financial liberalisation, and financial panic coupled with capital flight drove the economies down (Sachs 1998).

According to Little, Scitovsky and Scott, if a country needs to accelerate economic growth, the country needs to remove tariffs, quotas and other barriers to trade which distort relative prices and result in a misallocation of resources. The governments have to liberalise the banking and financial sectors since financial liberalisation allows free movement of capital (Little, Scitovsky and Scott 1970). However, during the 1997/98 crisis, countries that had liberalised their economies were the ones which were hit hardest. Market-oriented reforms were seen to be the main conduit through which the currency crisis infected the open economies of Southeast and East Asia (Kuttner 1998).

The process of globalisation is seen as the underlying reason for the economic woes of many of these countries. They are powerless to protect their economies against the large flow of capital, which create financial chaos in the process. The global economy therefore has to be reformed urgently (Kristof 1998).

During the 1990s, most industrialised countries were facing the problems of slow growth and a decline in interest rates. This phenomenon provided the impetus for the surge in capital flow to developing countries. Malaysia for example, was able to attract about 3.5% of the aggregate net resources flow to developing countries from 1990 to 1995 (Ong 1996).

There were both push and pull factors for the strong surge of capital flow to Malaysia. The push factors included the slow growth of the developed economies, the cyclical decline in international interest rates and the pressure for seeking higher rates of return. At the same time, pull factors included the strong economic fundamentals of Malaysia and growth potential due to political stability, a business-friendly government, attractive investment policies, adequate infrastructure, a booming stock market, high interest rates and expectations of ringgit appreciation (Ong 1996).

The massive inflow of foreign capital shifted the importance of sources of external finance for Malaysia. Official development finance declined in importance and foreign direct investment (FDI) and equity finance became much more substantial (Table 2.1).

2.6.2 Monetary Policy Against Capital Inflow

The Central Bank of Malaysia (Bank Negara Malaysia) took very strong and decisive monetary measures to control the excess liquidity in the banking system during the period of massive capital inflow. In the 1990-95 period, there were serious concerns over monetary instability, inflationary price pressure, asset price inflation and an overheating economy. Several policy options against capital inflow were taken by the government, including:

TABLE 2.1: ANNUAL CAPITAL INFLOWS BY MAJOR CATEGORY, 1989-95 (% OF GDP)

	1989	1990	1991	1992	1993	1994	1995
Current Account Balance	0.7	-2.1	-9.0	-3.8	-4.8	-6.3	-8.5
Net Capital Inflow	3.5	4.2	11.9	15.2	16.8	1.6	8.5
Official Development Finance	-2.4	-2.4	-0.5	-1.4	0.6	0.3	2.7
Foreign Direct Investment	4.4	5.4	8.5	9.0	7.8	6.0	4.7

Sources: National Accounts Statistics and Balance of Payment Report, Department of Statistics, Malaysia; BOP Reporting System, Bank Negara Malaysia.

- raising the statutory reserve requirement on bank funds
- centralising all government deposits placed with banking institutions with the Central Bank under Money Market Operation Account, which provided extra liquidity for the Central Bank to undertake open market operation, and
- direct borrowing from the inter-bank money market and locking in the perceived amount of excess liquidity with the sale of longer maturity monetary instruments (Ong 1996).

In 1992, two new administrative measures were introduced. First, a swap limit up to 2 million ringgit per customer was imposed on non trade-related swap transactions with non-residents by commercial banks. Second, bank deposits of the Employee Provident Fund amounting to US$2.6 billion were centralised with Bank Negara Malaysia (*BNM* 1992). In 1993, BNM created Treasury bills to mop up excess liquidity. In 1994, the Central Bank's open market operations had proven inadequate for addressing the task of sterilising the accelerating volume of portfolio capital inflow. As a result, the government had to look for more innovative ways of reducing the excessive liquidity. Capital inflow as well as unwanted speculative investment were discouraged. Several measures were introduced in 1994 to address these issues, including:

- raising the Statutory Reserve Requirement
- broadening the Eligible Liabilities Base for banking institutions
- prohibiting the sale of short-term monetary instruments to non-residents
- limiting foreign currency accounts with the central banks, and
- prohibiting swap transactions with non-residents.

The response to the Central Bank's 1994 monetary measures was mixed. There were arguments about the effects of the capital outflow from the country. There was substantial capital outflow in 1994 and it was argued that the subsequent outflow of speculative funds was partly due to the measures adopted by the government itself. The imposition of statutory reserve requirement on vostro accounts had driven away investors. To the Central Bank, the financial cost of implementing the tight monetary policy and monetary measures was indeed high.

On the other hand, the measures were successful in sustaining monetary stability from 1990 to 1996. Economic growth was not affected by the measures and the exchange rate of the ringgit was maintained. Between 1990 and 1995, the real exchange rate showed only showed a 5% appreciation (Ong 1996).

The above is an indication of Malaysian monetary policy in coping with massive capital inflow during 1990-95. The adequacy of the monetary policy in fighting the 1997/98 financial crisis was not addressed in the analysis. This crisis was unique compared to previous ones. The failure to shift from the existing monetary policy before 1 September 1998 to capital and selective exchange controls indicates a need for more innovative measures to cope with crises and to nurture ailing domestic industries.

Unlike the previous crisis in Malaysia which was sparked off by the public sector, the 1997 one was driven mainly by the private sector. Prior to that, most of the countries in this region had strong fundamentals – high saving-investment ratios, price stability, trade surpluses and high reserves. The difference was that there were the inflow of short-term capital, large current account deficits and the appreciation of exchange rates during the 1990s (Monte 1996).

2.7 Malaysia – Pre-Crisis Economic Weaknesses

2.7.1 The Pre-Crisis Boom

In 1993, the World Bank concluded that the East Asian economic growth (including that in Malaysia) was the result of export-oriented industrialisation, in contrast to the inward-oriented policies of less successful developing economies (World Bank 1993). The Asian Development Bank also concluded in its study that the main reasons for the fast growing East Asian economies was their ability to join the world economy by promoting labour-intensive manufactured exports (Asian Development Bank 1997).

Malaysia's boom was boosted by the massive redeployment of investment and production from developed countries, especially Japan. The Foreign Direct Investment (FDI) surge in

Malaysia was partly due to yen appreciation consequent to the Plaza Accord 1985 and the rising pressure for higher return of investment.

The Malaysian ringgit had appreciated in the early part of 1980s. However, it started depreciating in the second half of the decade, and continuing into the 1990s. Imports became more expensive. Though primary commodities prices fell in the first half of the 1980s, export prices and consequent increases in balance of payments deficit did not lower the real effective exchange rates of these currencies. The demand for the ringgit also increased due to a rise in heavy industry and infrastructure projects in Malaysia which Malaysia did not devalue the ringgit until 1985 (Rasiah 1994).

Following the strengthening of the Japanese Yen in 1986, the value of ringgit fell. The depreciating ringgit cheapened production cost in Malaysia as well as reduced the adverse effect of tariff deregulation in the country. Tariffs shielding import-substituting industries began to fall and export producers were enjoying subsidies. Thus the proportion of imports in final domestic demand did not soar in this period despite falling tariffs and despite some domestic industries having progressed (Rasiah 1994).

Malaysia had been making the effort to promote export-oriented manufacturing since the 1970s. The opening of free trade zones, investment incentives, greater equity ownership, tax exemptions and other measures had been introduced subsequently to attract more FDI. The increasing global demand and FDI redeployment led to the export surge.

2.7.2 CRONY VENTURES

Rapid growth in exports and the availability of resource rents helped the state to finance projects that favoured Bumiputera and other Malaysian businessmen. The aggressive moves of promoting stock markets, using both state guarantees and implicit assurances boosted confidence in the stock market. Foreign portfolio equity investment increased dramatically during the early 1990s.

The domestic markets were protected, which generated demand for monopolistic crony products and services in the country. The gains in rents were mere transfers from domestic consumers with options limited by tariffs, regulations and government procurement. Domestic demand grew even faster than export-oriented industries. Export-oriented interests began to move into real estate speculation and property development.

In general, Malaysia experienced massive increase in growth and structural change from the beginning of 1980 due to a combination of external forces and local initiatives. Cronyism piggy-backed the rapid growth without immediate debilitating consequences (Rasiah 2001).

2.7.3 THE 1997/98 FINANCIAL CRISIS

As pointed out by Rasiah (2001), weak economic fundamentals and poorly conceived liberalisation contributed to the financial crisis in Malaysia. There were various limitations on the country's capacity to improve and sustain competitiveness in international markets and efforts to strengthen the second order fundamentals could not be effective because of cronyism.

Another piece of research linked the 1997/98 financial crisis to financial liberalisation and the consequent undermining of effective financial regulation both at international and national levels (Chin & Jomo 2001).

Stiglits (1998 & 1999) pointed out that developing countries should be encouraged to find the appropriate regulatory structures or governance systems to manage the incentives and constraints which affect the exposure of financial institutions and their ability to cope with risk when engaged in rapid financial liberalisation.

There are also researchers who suggest that prudential regulation by the government is necessary to manage the trade-off between the competitive efficiency of markets and the security of the banking system (Park 1994; Chowdhury and Islam 1993).

Malaysia did not develop any well-conceived prudential regulatory instruments to manage portfolio investment inflow. She was ill equipped to deal with the currency and financial crisis, and with injudicious policy responses, had turned it into a crisis of the real economy (Jomo 1998).

Another pertinent comment is Krugman's, that the rapid growth of the Southeast Asian economies could not be sustained in the long run if the growth was generated by the increases in the factors of production rather than by increases in total factor productivity (Krugman 1998).

2.8 Malaysian Economic Recovery

2.8.1 Exports of Malaysia

One of the most important characteristics of Malaysia's robust economic development over the past few decades has been the openness of the economy to international trade and investment. This has led to the export sector becoming an important economic growth engine. From 1978 to 1997, the nominal value of gross exports grew at an average annual rate of 14% (Ong 1999). As shown in Table 2.2, the export sector of Malaysia is about 80% of GDP and manufactured exports represent 80% of the total exports (*BNM* 1998). According to the World Trade Organisation, Malaysia was the world's eighteenth largest export country in 1997. Two features characterise Malaysian exports. First, most of the manufactured exports are Foreign Direct Investment (FDI)-driven, and second, electronics and electrical goods dominate the Malaysian exports.

TABLE 2.2 COMPOSITION OF MALAYSIAN EXPORTS, 1997

Principal Exports	% of Total Exports
Manufactured Goods	**80.8**
Semiconductors	18.4
Electronic equipment & parts	18.1
Electrical machinery & appliances	17.2
Textile, clothing, footwear	3.4
Chemicals & chemical products	3.7
Wood products	2.9
Metals	2.6
Transport equipment	2.2
Rubber products	1.8
Agricultural Products	**10.5**
Rubber	1.3
Saw logs	1.1
Timber	1.3
Palm oil	4.9
Minerals	**7.0**
Crude oil	3.2
LNG	3.0
Tin	0.2
Other	**1.7**
% of GDP	**80.4**

Source: Department of Statistics, Bank Negara Malaysia, 1998 Annual Report.

2.8.2 EXPORT COMPETITIVENESS AND COMPARATIVE ADVANTAGE

Export competitiveness can be examined in a number of ways. According to the Theory of Comparative Advantage developed by Ricardo in 1817, export competitiveness is the ability to produce for export at a lower opportunity cost. Another argument of competitiveness is based on the Concept of Competitive Advantage developed by Porter (1990), where the emphasis is on the industry structure and government policy. The Concept of Competitive Advantage is akin to Krugman's (1994) strategic and managed trade.

To take advantage of the growth in demand, Malaysia needs to preserve the favourable supply conditions on which her competitive advantage is based. She needs to establish, and in fact has already established, a dynamic electronics industry through policies which provide competitive labour costs, productivity, and strategic location for both sourcing and marketing. Studies done by the National Productivity Corporation in Malaysia indicate continuing manufacturing efficiency in the electronics and electrical sector. At the same time, the currency depreciation during the 1997/98 financial crisis has improved price advantage. Hussain and Radelet (1999) calculated that the real exchange rate depreciated by 37.6%, putting the ringgit back at its 1990 competitive level. Malaysia's export competitiveness has been enhanced as a result of the crisis.

However, certain factors limited the actual gain in export business from such depreciation. Changes in bargaining power may accompany the decrease in currency value. At the same time, manufacturing companies operating at full capacity cannot expand production to benefit from the depreciated ringgit (Ong 1999).

2.8.3 The Export Sector's Contribution to Growth

From 1991 to 1997 Malaysia's net exports were negative due to large payments for freight and insurance which exceeded the trade balance. However, in 1998 the export sector contributed most to the economy. Net exports added 19.6% to GDP growth. The large contribution of the export sector came almost entirely from the contraction in imports rather than an increase in exports. Malaysia's experience in the Asian financial crisis indicates that reducing imports can make a contribution toward economic recovery (Ong 1999).

In response to the 1997/98 financial crisis, the Malaysian government set up a consultative body – the National Economic Action Council (NEAC). A comprehensive framework for economic recovery – the National Economic Recovery Plan (NERP) was implemented to stabilise the ringgit and restore stock market confidence. Besides the selective exchange and capital controls, NERP also addressed the close link between export and economic growth as part of the plan to strengthen the balance of payments. The measures comprised:

- promoting industries with low import content
- accelerating backward linkages for non-resource based industries and more local sourcing
- enhancing innovation of capital goods
- enhancing export-competitiveness of the manufacturing sector, and

- studying the cost-benefit of the electronics and electrical sectors.

Though Malaysia emphasises several export sectors, the government realised the downside risk of the external environment. Hence, the growth of the country had to be domestic-driven (Ong 1999).

2.9 RESEARCH GAPS, RESEARCH QUESTIONS AND RESEARCH PROPOSITIONS

The earlier sections provided a comprehensive review of the literature on related research issues, with most of the studies focusing on the causes of the 1997/98 currency crisis and the likely outcomes. Previous studies have highlighted the problems of the exchange rate regimes and the exchange controls which exist in the international exchange rate system. The review of the literature gave sharper focus on the issues and helped to identify the gaps in the body of knowledge. These are shown in Table 2.3.

2.9.1 RESEARCH QUESTIONS

The identified gaps in the body of knowledge underlined the need for the gathering of data to understand the research issues. The research questions related to the research issues are restated as follows:

- Is there a need for the currency and capital controls to insulate the Malaysian economy from the shortcomings of the global financial architecture?

- How innovative and appropriate are the currency and capital controls in addressing the problems of unfettered global currency flow?
- What is the response of both domestic and foreign investors to the currency and capital controls?
- How have currency and capital controls assisted in accelerating economic recovery in the country?
- Has the country's global competitive advantage benefited from the currency and capital controls?

TABLE 2.3: IDENTIFICATION OF RESEARCH GAPS

Research Issues	Literature Review Findings	Research Gaps
The need for exchange controls to overcome the shortcomings of the global financial architecture	No	The effectiveness of the Malaysian exchange control policy
Appropriateness of exchange controls to overcome the problems of currency flows • Global currency flows • Malaysian experience	 Yes No	The appropriateness of exchange controls in addressing the problem of unfettered currency flows
Impact on foreign and domestic investment	No	Influence of exchange controls on sentiments of both foreign and domestic investors
Impact on Malaysian economic recovery	No	Effectiveness of exchange controls in assisting Malaysian economic recovery
Impact on Malaysian global competitive advantage	No	Importance of exchange controls in enhancing global competitive advantage

Source: Derived from the Research Issue (Review)

2.9.2 RESEARCH OBJECTIVES

The research objectives explain the purpose of the research in measurable terms and specify what the research should achieve (Zikmund 1999). The objectives for this research are:

- To examine whether the currency and capital controls are necessary to insulate the Malaysian economy from the shortcomings of the global financial architecture
- To determine the extent to which capital and currency controls are innovative and appropriate in addressing the problems of unfettered global currency flows
- To determine how much Malaysian capital and currency controls have contributed to increased foreign and domestic investments
- To determine how capital and currency controls have helped accelerate economic recovery in the country, and
- To determine whether the Malaysian capital and currency controls enhanced the country's global competitive advantage.

2.9.3 RESEARCH PROPOSITIONS

Five research propositions have been formulated for testing by this research. These are:

- **RESEARCH PROPOSITION 1**

  That currency and capital controls are necessary to insulate the Malaysian economy from the shortcomings of the global financial architecture

- **RESEARCH PROPOSITION 2**
  That capital and currency controls are innovative and appropriate to address the problems of unfettered global currency flow
- **RESEARCH PROPOSITION 3**
  That the Malaysian capital and currency controls have contributed to increased foreign and domestic investments
- **RESEARCH PROPOSITION 4**
  That the Malaysian capital and currency controls have accelerated economic recovery in the country, and
- **RESEARCH PROPOSITION 5**
  That the Malaysian capital and currency controls have enhanced the country's global competitive advantage.

2.10 ASIAN CRISIS MANAGEMENT AND MALAYSIA

2.10.1 CURRENCY CRISIS IN MALAYSIA

In this section, theoretical points of view on the crisis and the Malaysian approach in crisis management will be examined. The analysis and description of measures undertaken by the Malaysian government in this section is a brief summary of Bank Negara Malaysia (Central Bank of Malaysia) *Annual Reports* for 1999, 2000 and 2001. Besides this, other sources are summarised here as well.

2.10.2 THE ASIAN CURRENCY CRISIS

Before the 1997/98 Asian Crisis, the strong economic growth of Asian countries was financed mainly by short-term capital and foreign debt. Much of the debt borrowed was unhedged and of short-term maturity. This short-term capital was pumped into speculative assets. The capital drove prices up, and some of this excess liquidity was also invested in large infrastructure projects. As a consequence, many of the companies had very high debt-to-equity ratios. (Refer Section 2.7)

When export growth was weakening, and the asset bubble appearing ready to burst, investors expected that the huge current account deficit and falling asset prices would finally lead to inability to service the foreign debt unless the currency was devalued. This was a fatal weakness that allowed speculators to attack the currency. The attack led to financial panic which spread to the stock market.

It is also believed that the growth of the country during the 1990s was inappropriately engineered and that the high growth of the country was partially due to speculative investment in properties and in the stock market. The short-term inflow of funds was reversible; therefore the growth was based on rather shaky foundations.

The banking systems in Asian countries were poorly supervised. Loan approval and risk ratings were poor. Furthermore, the mismatch of assets and liabilities of the banking sector worsened the situation. Most foreign funds borrowed by the banks were short-term, while the banks themselves lent out the money long-term. The sudden outflow of foreign funds forced the banks into insolvency. In addition, since most of the foreign investments were for speculative purposes, the value of the collateral to banks fell significantly when the investors pulled out their funds.

Corporate governance in these countries excepting Singapore and Hong Kong was quite inadequate. There was a lack of transparency and government bailout was very common. This created a scenario where moral hazards were widespread, with crony capitalism further fuelling the crisis. It is believed that the many crony-corporations were allowed to operate despite their not observing the market discipline.

The Southeast Asian countries embraced globalisation much too quickly and with inadequate preparation. They deregulated the financial system and removed restrictions on capital flow but maintained fixed exchange rates. This move contributed to the crisis.

2.10.3 Malaysia and the Currency Crisis

By the 1st quarter of 1997, the real exchange rate in Malaysia had appreciated about 15%. Over the previous ten years, capital inflow had been dominated by foreign direct investment (FDI). Starting from 1996, there had been a significant increase in the net inflow, driven by the boom in the Malaysian stock market. However, the appreciation also implies that the country's economic fundamentals may not be able to defend the currency from speculative attack (*BNM* 2000).

During the crisis, several intervention initiatives were taken by the Malaysian government in stock market operation, including the postponement of some infrastructure projects amounting to about US$10 billion. This further damaged investor confidence. Even the reform package unveiled on 5 December by the then Deputy Prime Minister and Finance Minister, Anwar Ibrahim, offered no concrete strategy for restructuring the financial system and raising the domestic interest rate to support the currency. Consequent to these developments and in order to boost market confidence, the government had to introduce even more new measures. Among them are:

1. Declaring on 28 August all the 100 component stocks of the KLCI as "designated securities" and announcing a RM60 billion standby facility to stabilise the stock market
2. Deferring all mega projects and cutting 1998 government spending by 18%
3. Reducing the balance of payments current account deficit from about 5 to 3% of GNP and revising the 1998 growth rate downwards from 7 to 4-5%, to reduce economic overheating
4. Freezing new share issues and corporate restructuring and banning corporate bailouts. Corporate buy backs were allowed, effective 1 September 1997 and
5. Increasing external reserves to cover 4 months of retained imports (BNM 2000).

Meanwhile, to strengthen both the economy and the banking system, Bank Negara Malaysia (BNM) introduced some precautionary measures (*BNM* 2000) such as:

1. Limiting non-commercial ringgit swap transactions with foreign bank customers to US$2 million per name per day
2. Slowing down loan growth from 25% in 1997 to 15% in 1998, and directing banking institution lending to productive sectors such as manufacturing and those activities that improve exports and foreign exchange earnings
3. Shortening the default period defining NPLs from 6 to 3 months and raising the general provision for bad and questionable debts from 1 to 1.5% of total loans and

4. Refraining from raising the domestic interest rate to strengthen the ringgit, despite the continuing depreciation of the currency.

There were some difficulties arising from the decision to restructure and recapitalise the banking system. It was not easy nor cheap obtaining funds for this purpose. BNM had to inject liquidity into the banking system by printing money. At that time as well, there was a conflict between the Prime Minister Dr. Mahathir Mohamed and his Deputy and Finance Minister Anwar Ibrahim. By mid 1998, the Malaysian government had only limited freedom in managing the crisis. Against this background, Dr. Mahathir then introduced his strategy of capital control and credit expansion.

The designed selective exchange control was targeted at reducing the internationalisation of the ringgit and stabilising capital inflow. The exchange control measures involved the following

1. Ringgit-denominated transactions among non-residents via external accounts required approval
2. The repatriation of portfolio capital had to be kept in Malaysia for at least one year
3. Both resident and non-resident travellers could import and export ringgit amounting to RM1,000 only
4. Malaysian investments abroad exceeding RM10,000 required approval and
5. Malaysians travelling abroad required approval to carry foreign currencies in excess of RM10,000 equivalent (*BNM* 2000).

Besides these measures, offshore banking was no longer allowed to trade in the ringgit instrument. Malaysian financial institutions could no longer offer domestic credit facilities to non-resident banks and stockbrokers, and the ringgit was fixed at RM3.8 per US dollar. This new fixed rate represented an appreciation of 10.5% against the market rate at the time, while the rate of depreciation against the pre-crisis rate was about 39%. There was no control on current account transactions, repatriation of profits, dividends, interest, fees, commission and rental income from portfolio investment and foreign direct investment (*BNM* 2000).

The capital control strategy was risky, because it allowed only temporary recovery through expansionary policies, which might lead to the postponement of long-term structural reforms, and thus to long-term economic deterioration. It involved economic costs associated with bureaucratic controls since prolonged use of controls tended to compound economic costs. The scope for avoidance was large since the economy of Malaysia was highly integrated in the world economy. Under this strategy, domestic inflation could be reflected in a real exchange rate appreciation. The cost of adjustment would fall disproportionately on the tradable sector, hindering an export-led recovery (Krugman 1998).

At the same time however, there were arguments for the measures, with suggestions that Malaysia had imposed the measures under carefully planned conditions. She did not impose control on all the transactions and the current account was still maintained open.

Following the imposition of these controls, Malaysia did not experience massive capital flight. The outflow of funds was mainly the prepayment of loans. Malaysia had in fact improved the current account before the imposition of the measures. External reserves before their implementation was sufficient to finance 4 months of imports. Furthermore, the short-term debt was just less than half of the reserves (*BNM* 2000).

Compared to other countries which have implemented capital controls, Malaysia's inflation rate was low. In the international market, Malaysia ranks favourably in terms of overall competitiveness and the relatively low price of exported goods have helped the nation to earn external reserves. It is believed that these factors contributed to the success of the measures. More importantly however, it earned the country some time for restructuring the domestic economy (*BNM* 2000).

2.10.4 Comparing the Recessions in 1985 and 1998

Both the recessions were triggered by external factors. In 1985, global decline in commodity prices and the subsequent slowdown in exports were the contributory factors. The slowdown in exports led to a cutback in private expenditure and deflationary pressure on the economy. The decline in aggregate demand affected the profitability of the corporates. Even the then booming property market was affected. At the same time, the problems in the financial sector eroded public confidence, especially after the failure of some deposit-taking cooperatives. By end 1988 non-performing loans (NPLs) had increased almost 30% (Samuel and Cheng 2000).

The 1998 recession was caused by the adverse development of the regional financial markets after the speculative attacks on the currencies of the East Asian countries. Despite the strong economic fundamentals, weak investor confidence and capital outflow caused the downward pressure on the stock market and the foreign exchange market. As the crisis prolonged, the aggregate demand fell, thus affecting the domestic economy and lowering the output level (Samuel and Cheng 2000).

The economic structure of Malaysia influenced both the depth and the magnitude of the two recessions. Although they were mainly due to external sources, the impact of shocks on the domestic economy was different, given the structural changes in economy.

In 1985, the Malaysian economy was vulnerable to fluctuations in world output and price of commodities. The government, accounting for 30.9% of total domestic demand, dominated the investments in the country. During the crisis, the implementation of counter-cyclical policies had led to deficits in both the fiscal and external payment positions, and there was also an increase in the external debt position (Samuel and Cheng 2000).

In 1998, the export sector remained vulnerable to the fluctuations in the international market. The differences were in product composition of exports and the diversification of markets. While commodities constituted the major export in 1985, it was electronics and electrical products that ranked highest in the 1998 list of exports (Samuel and Cheng 2000).

Besides this, alongside the process of globalisation, new risks had arisen from the free flow of capital. The sudden reversal of the capital flow and the contagion effect led to the crisis in the

1998 recession. The risk would have been higher if the current account deficit had been financed mainly by short-term capital flows rather than foreign direct investment.

As the major engine for growth shifted from the public to the private sector, new risks surfaced. Loans to the private sector increased to 148.4% of GDP in 1998 from 98.5% in 1990. Most of these loans were collateralised against properties and shares. The danger was the depreciation of the asset prices, which would eventually increase the risks in the banking system (Samuel and Cheng 2000).

2.10.5 Monetary Policy during Recessions

In 1985, the expansionary monetary policy was aimed at reviving economic growth, and achieved through easing bank liquidity while containing upward pressure on interest rates. However, the efforts were neutralised to a large degree by outflow of funds. In 1997-1998, the situation was almost the same. The difference was in the magnitude of the speculative activities. Due to the availability of a large amount of ringgit funds abroad, the effectiveness of the monetary policy was limited as speculative disruption in the foreign exchange market played down their effectiveness. In late 1997, the monetary policy was tightened to contain inflation and restore stability in the foreign exchange market. However, this tightening only slowed down aggregate demand in the economy. The easing of the monetary policy and the measures to improve the banking sector was achieved only after the implementation of selective exchange controls (Rasiah 2001).

In both crises, banking institutions had not performed their role of intermediation well. The intermediation process was inefficient, the cost of funds high and the adjustment of the base lending rate slow. As a result, the government had to introduce measures to improve the efficiency of the market. In 1985, the authorities suspended the market determination of interest rates and pegged them to the base-lending rate. The 1998 measures were mainly aimed at improving liquidity in the market, as well as to ensure more transparent management in the banking system (Samuel and Cheng 2000).

2.10.6 Fiscal Policy during Recessions

There were differences in the fiscal policy adopted by the government in dealing with the two recessions. The policy in 1985 was mainly focused on fiscal restraint. It reduced expenditure leading to the fiscal deficit increasing to 11.2% of GDP the following year.

Before the 1998 recession, the healthy fiscal position of fiscal surplus and low external debts provided the government greater freedom in employing fiscal policy. At the beginning of the crisis in 1997, the government pursued a prudent fiscal policy. However, the severity of the slowdown prompted a switch to counter-cyclical fiscal measures. Expenditure was directed to the private sector, which could lead to the maximisation of the multiplier effect on economic activities (Samuel and Cheng 2000).

The Malaysian government took several important measures to overcome the problems of capital outflow, as well as internal structural problems. Many possible factors have been identified, and while none of the factors could have, by themselves, caused the financial crisis, they were in fact interrelated. In order to find out the effectiveness of the controls, it is necessary to go back to the performance of the fundamentals of the economy as is reflected in the economic statistics. The analysis in the following section reveals the economic performance after the imposition of the controls.

2.11 ECONOMIC PERFORMANCE

2.11.1 MALAYSIAN ECONOMIC PERFORMANCE

After 12 years of uninterrupted growth, the Malaysian economy had for the first time declined to a crisis level. Adjustment measures were taken but they could not restore stability in the market. This factor, coupled with the decline in both international and domestic demand and the continued waves of adjustment in currency and stock markets, put the economy in recession. This prompted the government to implement an expansionary policy which was contradictory to the one designed by the IMF (tight fiscal policy and tight monetary policy).

To promote growth and recovery, the National Economy Action Council set up a comprehensive National Economy Recovery Plan. From May 1998, both the fiscal and the monetary policies were relaxed to counter the cyclical effect and to avoid a recession-deflation spiral. However, external factors such as political problems in Indonesia, devaluation of the rouble and the weakening Japanese yen led to the depreciation of the ringgit by 40% against the US dollar and a decline in the stock market by about 72% from pre-crisis level. Starting from 1 September, Malaysia imposed selective exchange controls to eliminate internationalisation of the ringgit and to stabilise capital flow. With the implementation of all these measures and the consequent improved liquidity in the domestic market, the government could then take further action to improve the banking system and to increase bank lending.

The imperfections of the international monetary system in dealing with short-term flow led to the financial crisis in 1997/98. Herd behaviour and the misperception of international investors as well as rating agencies led to market expectations becoming self-fulfilling. In fact, the downward risks in the Malaysian economy at the time were the high loan-to-GDP ratio, growing credit, and the deficit in current account. Overall, people agreed that Malaysia had stronger fundamentals. However, they did not differentiate the risks among the countries in this region.

The analysis in this chapter is a brief summary of Bank Negara Malaysia (Central Bank of Malaysia) Annual Reports years 2000 and 2001. The statistics and numeric figures in this chapter also rely heavily on data from the Ministry of Finance, the National Economic Action Committee and the Department of Statistics.

2.11.2 GDP GROWTH

As Figure 2.1 indicates, the GDP growth rate at purchasers' price was at 7.3% in 1997, -7.4% in 1998, 5.8% in 1999 and 8.5% in 2000. Factors such as uncertainty in economic outlook and employment prospects, deferment of projects, and negative wealth effects resulted in a decline in private sector spending. The decline in aggregate demand led to the problems of overcapacity and build-up in stocks, all of which further depressed private investment (BNM 2001).

The imposition of exchange controls in September 1998 improved market sentiment. This is reflected in the Business Conditions Index of MIER (Table 2.4). On an annual basis, the real GDP declined tremendously, while in a preceding quarter, the real GDP had improved since the 2nd quarter of the year.

FIGURE 2.1: GDP GROWTH RATE

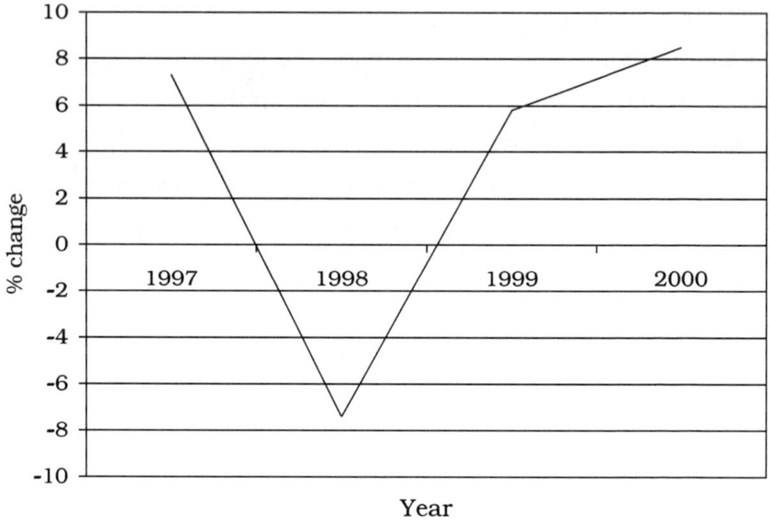

Source: Department of Statistics, Malaysia Year 2001

The real output growth in 1999 rose to 9.4% in the second half-year due to expansionary fiscal and monetary policies. Both factors of positive external developments and the prompt policy response to the 1997/8 crisis produced the better-than-expected performance in 1999. World growth also improved to 3% in 1999 (2.5% in 1998) due to the recovery of the Asian countries and higher growth in industrial countries. The higher growth rates both in the domestic and international markets contributed to increased demand. On the domestic front, the imposed selective exchange controls eliminated the internationalisation of the ringgit. This in turn enabled the government to take proactive measures to bring about recovery to the country. The imposed exchange controls provided businesses with the degree of certainty essential for planning their operations. Other than that, the stable condition also encouraged exports and foreign investment. Coupled with the fiscal stimulus package and strengthened financial sector, expansion in export-oriented industries improved domestic private consumption (*BNM* 2001).

TABLE 2.4: SECTORAL PERFORMANCE

	Annual change (%)			
Year	**1997**	**1998**	**1999**	**2000**
GDP	7.3	-7.4	5.8	8.5
Agriculture	0.7	-3.3	3.8	0.4
Mining	1.9	0.8	-3.1	-0.5
Manufacturing	10.1	-13.4	13.5	21.0
Construction	10.6	-23.0	-5.6	1.1
Services	9.9	-0.7	3.3	4.7

Source: Department of Statistics, Malaysia Year 2001.

The real output growth in 1999 rose to 9.4% in the second half-year due to expansionary fiscal and monetary policies. Both factors of positive external developments and the prompt policy response to the 1997/8 crisis produced the better-than-expected performance in 1999. World growth also improved to 3% in 1999 (2.5% in 1998) due to the recovery of the Asian countries and higher growth in industrial countries. The higher growth rates both in the domestic and international markets contributed to increased demand. On the domestic front, the imposed selective exchange controls eliminated the internationalisation of the ringgit. This in turn enabled the government to take proactive measures to bring about recovery to the country. The imposed exchange controls provided businesses with the degree of certainty essential for planning their operations. Other than that, the stable condition also encouraged exports and foreign investment. Coupled with the fiscal stimulus package and strengthened financial sector, expansion in export-oriented industries improved domestic private consumption (*BNM* 2001).

The GDP for year 2000 increased by 8.5%. This strong growth was prompted by the adjustment in the banking system and in the financial markets. The ringgit exchange rate was estimated to be marginally undervalued during the first half of the year and closed to near equilibrium level by year-end. Such strong fundamentals allowed the government to set a policy which was resilient to external shocks (*BNM* 2001).

2.11.3 Sectoral Review

In 1998, almost all sectors had been affected, except the mining sector. The construction sector declined in output by 24.5%, manufacturing 10.2% and agriculture 4%. Demand for services also reduced, evidenced by the decline in wholesale and retail trade, hotel, restaurants and other sub-sectors (*BNM* 2001).

In 1999 growth was driven by export-oriented industries in the manufacturing sector. Starting from the second quarter of the year, both domestic and export-oriented industries registered positive growth rates. In the second quarter, all sectors except mining and construction registered positive growth rates. By the third quarter, mining was the only sector that did not register positive growth rate (*BNM* 2001).

Real output expanded by 10% in the first half of year 2000 and the export of manufactured goods increased by 19.1% in the first half of the year. The strong export growth was due to the sustained strong demand for electronics and electrical products and the expansion of oil-based exports. Even with the moderation in global growth rate, the export of manufactured goods was sustained at 23.9% in the third quarter and 7% in the fourth quarter (*BNM* 2001).

As shown in Table 2.4 and Figure 2.2, almost all the important sectors portrayed the same trend as the GDP. The exception was the manufacturing sector which registered high growth rate after the third quarter of 1998. The strong growth was driven not just because of strong demand from international markets but also partially due to the stable exchange rate after the imposition of exchange controls.

2.11.4 DOMESTIC DEMAND

For the first time in 12 years, aggregate domestic demand declined in 1998. The adjustment and downward movement of both the currency and stock market, together with the effect of balance sheet adjustments and weak external demand contributed to the contraction of private investment and consumption. In the first three quarters of the year, aggregate domestic demand declined by 20.6% in current prices (Figure 2.3). This can be compared with the previous year when the growth rate was 9.6%, and with the average annual growth rate of about 13.5% in the period 1987-97. In real terms, the decline in domestic expenditure was about 25.9% (*BNM* 2001).

Total consumption spending declined by 6.5% in nominal terms, although in real terms, it declined by 10.3%. Uncertain employment prospects, inflationary pressure and a decline in share prices led to more cautious spending. Total loans approved by the banking institutions for personal use and for purchasing consumer goods declined by 72.2% and 93.6% respectively. Public consumption expenditure also declined by 1.5% in nominal terms and 3.5% in real terms. The moderate decline in public consumption expenditure was the result of the contractionary measures taken by the government in the fourth quarter of 1997. However, in the second half of 1998, the government reversed the fiscal policy by adopting an expansionary fiscal policy aimed at pre-empting further contraction in domestic demand (*BNM* 2001).

FIGURE 2.2: SECTORAL PERFORMANCE (BASE: 1987)

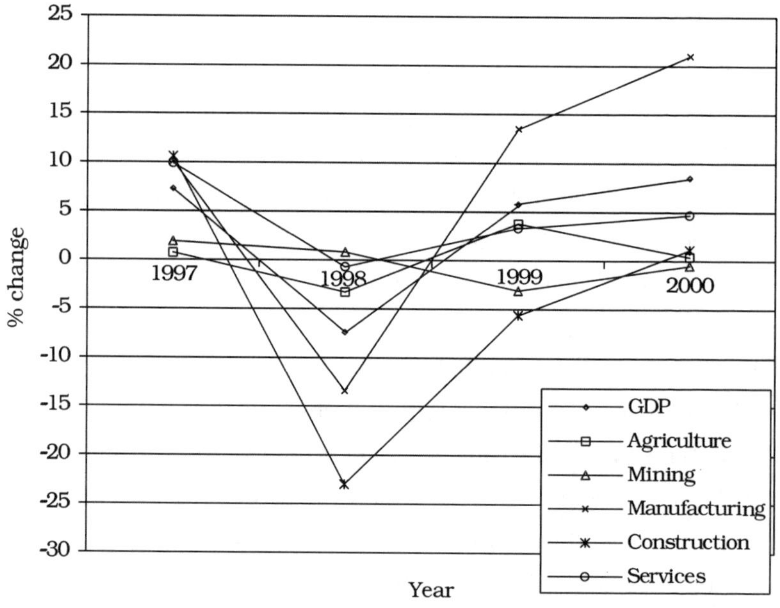

Source: Department of Statistics, Malaysia Year 2001

FIGURE 2.3: GNP AT CURRENT PURCHASERS' PRICES

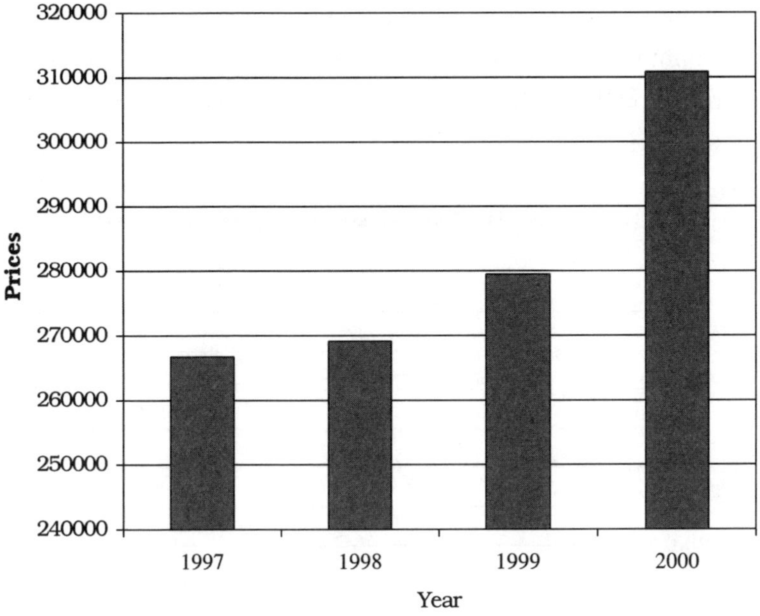

Source: Department of Statistics, Malaysia Year 2001

The contraction in total investment was higher, at 39% in nominal terms and 44.9% in real terms (Figure 2.4). Private investment declined by 53.3% in nominal terms. Import of capital goods declined significantly. Loans extended by banking institutions to the property sector increased by 5.3% and those to the manufacturing sector declined by 0.2% in 1998. Circumstances however improved from September 1998 onwards (*BNM* 2001).

Besides this, the structural changes in the economy and the uncertainty in the market caused a 38% decline in investment in the manufacturing sector. This decline affected both the domestic and export-oriented industries. Foreign investors deferred their investment due to weak export demand and less favourable developments in developing countries. The value of investment approved by the MITI in 1998 however recorded an increase of 2.3% (*BNM* 2001)

FIGURE 2.4: SAVINGS-INVESTMENT GAP

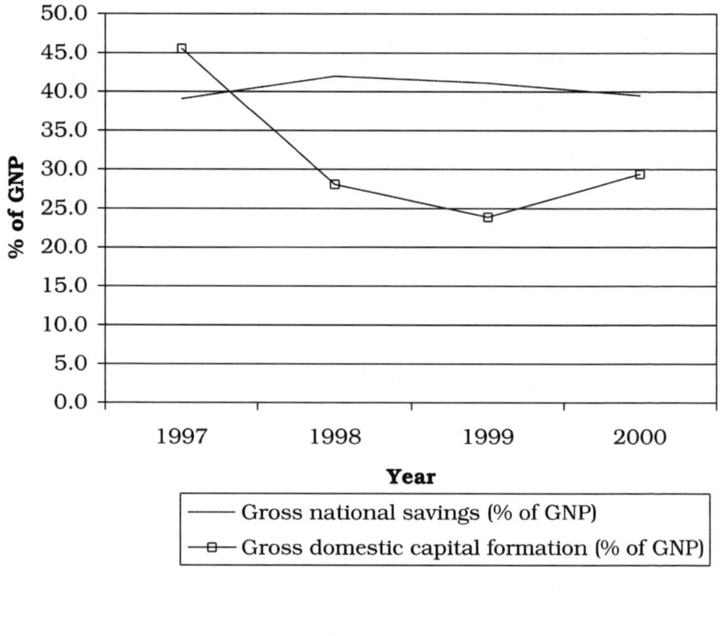

Source: Department of Statistics, Malaysia Year 2001

Growth in real aggregate domestic demand (excluding stocks) turned positive from the third quarter of 1999. The growth in aggregate demand was mainly the result of higher government expenditure and the revival in private sector consumption. Private investment in the year was low due to excess capacity. Overall, aggregate domestic demand (excluding stocks) registered a positive growth of 1.2% in nominal terms and 1.6% in real terms (*BNM* 2001).

Total consumption expenditure increased by 8.4% in nominal terms in 1999 (-7.4% in 1998). In real terms, total consumption spending improved by 6.1% (-10.2% in 1998). Public consumption increased by 20% in nominal terms and 20.1% in real terms. Private consumption expenditure turned around to record a positive growth of 5.6% in nominal terms and 2.5% in real terms for 1999 (*BNM* 2001).

Public investment expenditure increased by 3.1% in nominal terms and 10.1% in real terms in 1999. Consistent with the fiscal stimulus programme, the allocation for socio-economic projects and selected infrastructure projects was increased. Private investment continued to decline, but at a slower rate of –24.1% in nominal terms and –19% in real terms in 1999 compared to 1998 (–50.5% and –55% respectively). Import of capital goods in US dollar terms declined by 40.5% in 1998 and 25.1% in the first half-year in 1999, but increased by 16.7% in the second half of 1999. Overall, investment activities were stronger in the agriculture and mining sectors (*BNM* 2001).

The saving-investment gap at RM47.4 billion remained in surplus for the second consecutive year (RM36.8 billion in 1998). As private consumption recovered, savings declined 0.1%. The public sector recorded a slightly higher surplus of RM12.6 billion. Gross National Savings (GNS) increased at a slower rate of 1.4% in 1999.

The momentum of domestic aggregate demand grew in 2000. The government's expansionary fiscal policy strengthened consumer and investor sentiment. The growth of real aggregate domestic demand accelerated to 14.6%.

Public investment expenditure increased at a higher rate of 21.7% in real terms. Higher spending was channelled into the education and health sectors. Expenditure on emoluments and supplies of the Federal Government increased strongly in 2000.

Due to improved sentiment, private sector expenditure rebounded strongly. The overall growth was at 15.7%. Private consumption sustained at 12.4%. The reduction of personal income tax and upward adjustment of salaries contributed to increased consumption in the year.

Private investment activities gained momentum as well. Total investment increased by 26.7%. The increasing investment activities also triggered more loans disbursement within the banking system (*BNM* 2001).

2.11.5 Balance of Payments

The balance of payments was better then expected especially in the speed and the magnitude of the current account adjustment. The current account recorded a surplus of RM36.1 billion in 1998 compared to a deficit of RM14.2 in 1997 (See Figure 2.5). This surplus was mainly due to the depreciated ringgit, the favourable valuation on the export earnings and the decline in imports. It recorded a large surplus in the merchandise account, which offset the deficit in both the service account and the outflow of the transfer account (*BNM* 2001).

FIGURE 2.5: BALANCE ON CURRENT ACCOUNT AS % OF GNP

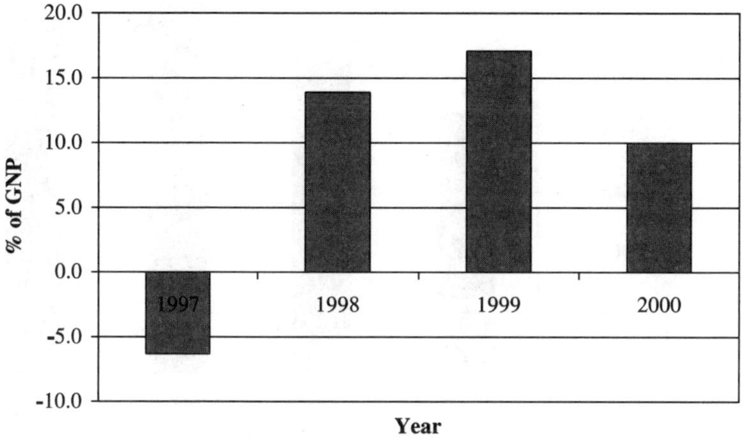

Source: Department of Statistics, Malaysia and Bank Negara Malaysia Year 2001

The balance of payments position strengthened in 1999 due to the strong improvement in net exports and capital inflow. The surplus of balance of payments at RM17.8 billion led to higher external reserves of RM117.2 billion (US$30.9 billion) (Figure 2.6). The current account was stronger than that in the previous year, reflecting better export performance despite increasing imports. Imports had been limited to a certain extent by a government policy aimed at reducing imports and employing content from the domestic market. The surplus in current account also offset the effect of short-term capital outflow. The inflow of funds into the country, comprising official long-term capital and foreign direct investment, were offset by the outflow from Malaysian investment abroad (*BNM* 2001).

FIGURE 2.6: INTERNATIONAL RESERVES (US$)

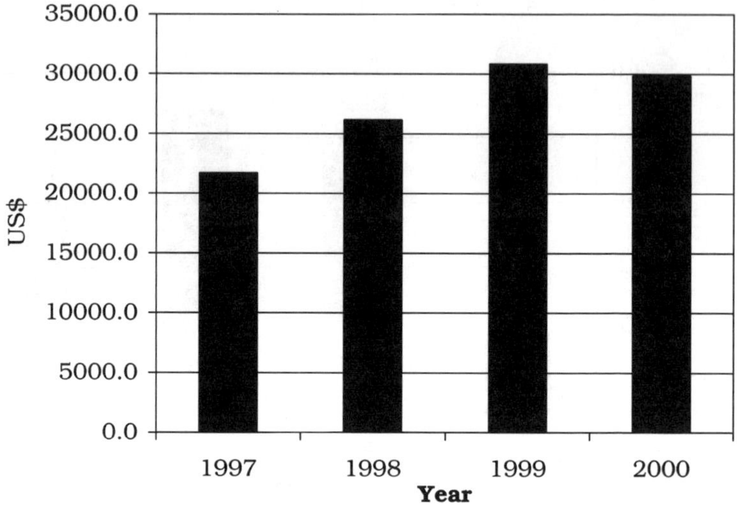

Source: Department of Statistics, Malaysia and Bank Negara Malaysia Year 2001

There was a large surplus in the trade balance and sustained inflow of long-term capital. The strong balance of payments benefited from higher oil prices. The stable exchange rate also enabled industries to increase their export-oriented output. The current account remained strong and recorded a larger surplus for the year. However, this was still lower than the surplus in the previous year because of higher imports.

2.11.6 FISCAL AND MONETARY POLICIES

In 1998, the Malaysian government imposed an expansionary fiscal policy in order to avoid a deeper contraction of domestic aggregate demand. From August of that year, it started to employ monetary policy together with an expansionary fiscal policy, thereby achieving increased market liquidity, lowering the cost of financing, stabilising investment sentiment and improving consumer sentiment.

In 1999 selective exchange controls imposed the year before eliminated the internationalisation of the ringgit. This enabled the government to take proactive measures to bring about recovery to the country. The imposed exchange controls provided businesses with a degree of certainty with which to plan their operations. Other than that, the stable condition also encouraged exports and foreign investment. Coupled with the fiscal stimulus package, the strengthened financial sector and expansion in export-oriented industries improved domestic private consumption.

Malaysia's macroeconomic policy in 1999 focused on strengthening the recovery process and on implementing the restructuring process. In early 1999, the recovery was at an initial stage and there were still uncertainties about the prospects for growth in industrial countries. There was also excess capacity. The policy was designed in such a way that domestic demand could be strengthened through fiscal stimulus. At the same time, the government also recognised the negative effect of a budget deficit. Therefore, the government maintained the deficit at a level that would not jeopardise public sector policies in the long term.

Government priority in spending was directed to projects related to social-economic and structural issues. Furthermore, the stimulus package was implemented in a way that minimised leakage abroad while the expenditure was financed largely from domestic sources (69%). External debts raised during the year were mainly from raising global bonds and funding obtained from multilateral sources such as the World Bank and the Islamic Development Bank (*BNM* 2001).

In the absence of inflationary pressure, the monetary policy was relaxed to support the expansionary fiscal policy during 1999. The easing of monetary policy provided ample liquidity. The interest rate was lowered and the resulting reduction in the cost of funds provided banking institutions with the flexibility to reduce lending rates.

Believing that growth is slow in industrial countries, the Malaysia macroeconomic management in 2000 focused on sustaining domestic demand. Along with this, the long-term macroeconomic strategy continued to maintain stability of the economy.

To maintain sustainable economic growth, Malaysia emphasised an expansionary fiscal policy. The fiscal stimulus package included both non-tax and tax measures. The measures included tax relief, reduction of personal income tax rate, salary adjustment for government servants and the reduction of import duties on certain consumer goods. Incentives were also given to encourage house ownership. In the meantime, the government encouraged quality investment into targeted sectors.

Priority in government expenditure was allocated to education, skills training, rural development, agriculture, low-cost housing, industrial and infrastructure development and health services. The fiscal deficit was largely financed from non-inflationary domestic sources. Only about 6.4% of net funds raised by the government was from the international capital market (*BNM* 2001).

Monetary policy remained accommodative to support the strengthening of economic activities. Low interest rates led to growth in bank lending. The low interest rates and the pegged exchange rate ensured stability in market conditions. Throughout the year, loans outstanding increased, driven mainly by higher credit growth in both households and businesses. Loans outstanding increased by 5.4% at the end of 2000. Bank Negara Malaysia monitored the banking sector closely, ensuring that firms were limited in exposure to the property sector and the purchase of shares (*BNM* 2001).

2.11.7 Banking and Corporate Restructuring

Banking institutions were encouraged to channel funds to viable activities to support the economic recovery. In 1999, loan approvals averaged RM8.7 billion a month (RM5.4 billion a month in 1998) and disbursements recorded an average of RM26.9 billion a month (RM20.9 billion a month in 1998). The marginal increase of 0.3% in total outstanding loans of the banking system reflected developments such as high repayments, writing-off of loans and the conversion of loans to bonds (*BNM* 2001).

Bank Negara Malaysia expended a lot of effort to restructure the banking sector. Recognising that there is over-reliance on the banking institutions to finance the economy, the development of the bond market was accelerated. In June 1999, a National Bond Market Committee (NBMC) was established to provide overall policy and support for the orderly development of the market.

Malaysia also accelerated the pace of corporate restructuring and banking sector restructuring. By 31 December 1999, Danaharta (a national asset management company), which was set up in June 1998, had acquired and managed NPLs totalling RM45.5 billion from the financial sector. Of this RM35.7 billion was from the banking sector. The NPL level in the banking sector reduced to 6.6% based on 6-month classification as at 31 December 1999. In order to acquire the NPLs, Danaharta issued RM10.3 billion nominal value bonds up to December 1999. By then, Danaharta had achieved a recovery rate of 80.2% on the loans and assets that it had restructured (*BNM* 2001).

Danamodal, the bank recapitalisation agency set up in August 1998, had injected RM7.1 billion into 10 banking institutions to recapitalise the affected banks. The amount of capital injected had been reduced to RM5.3 billion by end January 2000 (*BNM* 2001).

The success of both Danaharta and Danamodal spurred Bank Negara Malaysia to strengthen the banking sector through mergers and consolidation. The merger exercise was expected to be completed by end-December 2000. The aim was to create a resilient, efficient and competitive banking sector.

The selective exchange control measures that were implemented in September 1998 were liberalised after they had achieved their objectives. Instead of holding portfolio capital for at least one year in Malaysia, foreign investors were then allowed to repatriate principal capital and profits, subject to a graduated levy. Following the implementation of the system, there was a net inflow of funds from non-residents amounting to RM4 billion, which was mainly channelled into the stock market.

During the year 2000, both domestic and foreign banking institutions were required to keep minimum capital funds. Domestic banks were required to increase to RM2 billion and foreign banks RM300 million.

On the corporate side, corporate governance, transparency, minority shareholders protection and accounting standards were enforced to protect the shareholders.

Included in this effort was the establishment of a Minority Shareholders Watchdog Group.

Financial institutions also continued their consolidation programme. 50 out of 54 banking institutions were consolidated into 10. Tax incentives were provided to accelerate mergers and consolidation. As a result, 94% of total assets of the domestic banking institutions had been rationalised and consolidated (*BNM* 2001).

By the time Danaharta completed its acquisition exercise, RM37.5 billion of NPLs had been removed from the banking sector. Danaharta had successfully restructured RM35.8 billion of loans while another RM23.8 billion of NPLs was expected to be recovered (*BNM* 2001).

2.11.8 Secondary Data Analysis

The secondary data provide a meaningful insight on the economic performance of Malaysia. From the analysis, certain research propositions have been answered. The research propositions are subsequently restated, as follows:

> **RESEARCH PROPOSITION 1:** The currency and capital controls are necessary to insulate the Malaysian economy from the shortcomings of the global financial architecture.
>
> Secondary data analysis shows that the currency and capital controls were important for the process of economic recovery. The strong growth of GDP after the imposition of controls serves as strong evidence of the effectiveness of the controls. However, there is no evidence to show that the improved domestic demand was due to the exchange controls.

Research Proposition 1 is therefore accepted according to the secondary data analysis. The exchange controls were needed to insulate the Malaysian economy from the shortcomings of the global financial architecture.

RESEARCH PROPOSITION 2: The capital and currency controls are innovative and appropriate to address the problems of unfettered global currency flows.

Capital liberalisation is good for a developing economy with a sound financial system. However, massive capital inflow may lead to an economic bubble. Furthermore, it may lead to a current-account deficit. Secondary data analysis indicates that the controls were suitable in the short run. The controls allowed Malaysia to re-engineer the domestic economy. The fixed exchange rate enabled Bank Negara Malaysia to keep interest rates low while the capital control enabled the country to avoid massive capital outflow. Research Proposition 2 is there fore supported by the secondary data.

RESEARCH PROPOSITION 3: The Malaysian capital and currency controls have contributed to increased foreign and domestic investments.

The secondary data analysis indicates that both the domestic and foreign private investments were declining after the crisis and the subsequent imposition of the capital control. There were many factors that affected investor confidence. These factors are examined in the primary data analysis.

The research proposition is not accepted from the information generated for the secondary data analysis. The findings suggest that the controls have not contributed to increased domestic and foreign investments.

RESEARCH PROPOSITION 4: The Malaysian capital and currency controls have assisted in speedy economic recovery in the country.

The analysis indicates that there was economic recovery in the country. However, there are two indicators of recovery that are not evident. They are structural reforms of financial institutions and restoration of investor confidence.

The empirical facts suggest that the proposition is accepted as the controls have assisted in speedy economic recovery. However, the world economic downturn since late 2000 has blurred the effectiveness of the controls imposed by the Malaysian government.

RESEARCH PROPOSITION 5: The Malaysian capital and currency controls will enhance the country's global competitive advantage.

The findings indicate that ringgit has been undervalued. However, regional currency depreciation affects the relative value of ringgit in international markets. Thus, the imposed pegged rate affects the competitiveness of the country.

Research proposition 5 is not accepted as the evidence indicates that the controls have led to deterioration of the competitiveness of the country.

2.11.9 CONCLUSION

This chapter reviewed and discussed the following:

- The definitions and the evolution of the exchange rate systems and the criteria of exchange rate regimes under different systems (Section 2.2)
- Exchange rate systems in East Asia, the UK, the US and the European Union; the relationship between exchange rate regimes and the recovery of the Asian financial crisis (Section 2.3)
- Global experiences of exchange controls, which included capital and exchange controls (Section 2.4)
- The Malaysian pre-crisis economic weaknesses (Section 2.5) and the Malaysian experience of capital flow and monetary policy (Section 2.6)
- Malaysian capital and exchange controls, and economic recovery plan (Section 2.7 and 2.8)
- Research gaps which could be bridged with the research (Section 2.9), and
- The crisis management by the Malaysian government and the policies that responded to the crisis and the outcomes of the policies (Section 2.10 and 2.11).

Based on these findings the next chapter will deal with the Research Methodology to be employed in examining the Research Propositions.

RESEARCH METHODOLOGY

3.1 INTRODUCTION

In this chapter, an appropriate methodology for the research is identified. In order to do so, a clear perception of research activities and a good understanding of data theory are required.

As there is little literature on the research problems, it is necessary to have in-depth understanding of the dimensions of the problems. This is done through exploratory research. Again, since not much study has been conducted in this area, extensive interviews are necessary for better understanding of the situation and the phenomena (Zikmund 1999).

The research commenced with the literature review on exchange rate systems as set out in Chapter 2. It gives a detailed review of the literature to develop the issues and to formulate the following research propositions:

- The currency and capital controls were necessary to insulate the Malaysian economy from the shortcomings of the global financial architecture

- The capital and currency controls were innovative and appropriate to address the problems of unfettered global currency flows
- The Malaysian capital and currency controls have contributed to increased foreign and domestic investments
- The Malaysian capital and currency controls have assisted in the speedy economic recovery in the country, and
- The Malaysian capital and currency controls have enhanced the country's global competitive advantage.

Secondary data analysis was carried out to piece the picture together. The current situation is described in Chapter 2.10 and 2.11. Economic performance for the period from 1998 to 2000 was reviewed for a better understanding of the economic development during and after the exchange crisis.

Following the literature review and secondary data analysis, primary data was collected for the testing of the research propositions. The primary data collection consisted of a questionnaire survey of 200 companies and in-depth interviewing with policy makers, some 30-40 industrialists who had been affected by the capital controls. The companies were selected based on the overall rating obtained by adding the individual ratings from four viewpoints: the stability of dividend and earnings, financial strength, management strength and future growth of dividend/ earnings.

Section 3.2 examines the different research categories and justification for the selection of exploratory research in the context of data theory. Section 3.3 comprises the exploratory research selected methods. Data collection techniques and the conduct of focus group interviews are explained in Section 3.4 while Section 3.5 is devoted to data analysis procedures. Section 3.6 presents the conclusion of the research methodology.

3.2 JUSTIFICATION FOR THE PREFERRED METHODOLOGY

The discussions in the sections comprise three main parts. First is the data theory and theory building. The next is the types of research and the adopted research design while the final part concentrates on the methodology and instruments for data collection and analysis.

3.2.1 PERSPECTIVES ON DATA THEORY

The purpose of research is to expand knowledge and discover the truth. Research contributes to theory building, where "a theory is a coherent set of general propositions used to explain the apparent relationships among certain observed phenomena" (Zikmund 1999). Theory can be developed through inductive or deductive reasoning.

Inductive research methods, or an interpretative research paradigm are appropriate for situations with a relatively under-developed theory base (Yin 1989). Deductive reasoning on the other hand is the logical process of deriving a conclusion from a known premise or from something known to be true (Zikmund 1999).

Inductive approaches are more subjective, idiographic, insider in nature and quantitative (Parke 1993). While positivist research methods have dominated management research, more recent authorities have tended to advocate the interpretative paradigm (Mannen 1982). There are several reasons for this move away from positivist methods. First of all, deductive analysis methods result in theory development without the benefit of informed data. Also, there is not much predictive value from positivist research methods. Thirdly, qualitative research is more suitable for exploring and discovery in an era of rapid and fundamental change.

As Marsick (1990) suggested, inductive research methods are useful for building new theory and for exploring uncharted territory. Thus qualitative approaches are appropriate for this research.

3.2.2 Categories of Business Research

Business research is concerned with data acquisition and analysis. Basically research can be grouped into three main categories (Zikmund 1999):

1. Pure research which is largely concerned with theoretical concepts for extending the boundaries of knowledge
2. Applied research, which focuses on primary information to answer questions on specific problems and is best suited for decision-making and formulating policy approaches, and
3. Evaluation research, a formal objective measurement which appraises the extent to which a given activity, project or programme has achieved its objective (Zikmund, 1999).

This research is mainly designed to find the answer for the currency crisis, a specific problem seeking answers for decision-making and formulating approaches. It therefore falls into the category of applied research.

3.2.3 Types of Research Methods

There are several types of research methods that may be used for research studies (Zikmund 1999).

1. "Exploratory Research" is research conducted to clarify and define the nature of the research problems. It helps to crystallise and identify information for future research
2. "Descriptive Research" is specifically designed to describe characteristics of population or a phenomenon. It need not explain the causes. Accuracy is very important.
3. "Diagnostic Analysis" is used to understand findings, such as explaining behaviour and attitude of respondents and is closely aligned to descriptive research, and
4. "Causal Research" is best suited for the identification of cause and effect relationships among variables. Usually, the problem of the research is narrowly defined.

3.2.4 Justification for Exploratory Research

Exploratory research is important for advancing knowledge through theory building, where not too much is known about the research problem. It is the preferred type to comprehend the nature of the problem to enable more rigorous research to be undertaken subsequently (Zikmund 1999).

According to Perry (1995) "Time and resource constraints necessitate the choice of only one major research methodology which is suited to the research problem." This study is subject to two principle constraints:

1. Time and resources constraints, and

2. Inadequacy of secondary data on the unforeseen financial crisis of 1997/98. Little research has been undertaken on the implications of the newly-introduced capital controls in the Malaysian economy.

These factors excluded the use of a quantitative research method. Although it was recognised that exploratory research may lead to subjective judgmental interpretation of the findings, this method was nevertheless considered the most appropriate.

3.2.5 RESEARCH DESIGN

In order to conduct meaningful research, a careful planning of inter-related activities for an orderly investigation is required. It involves systematic and objective processes for gathering, recording and analysing data (Zikmund 1999).

A range of activities was arranged to define the research problem. As Figure 3.1 shows, it involved six steps:

1. Ascertaining the research objectives
2. Understanding the background of the problem
3. Isolating and identifying the problem rather than its symptoms
4. Determining the unit of analysis

    - The Malaysian economy as a whole
    - The Malaysian public-listed companies, and
    - Government officials

5. Determining the relevant variables, and
6. Stating the research questions and objectives.

FIGURE 3.1 THE PROCESS OF PROBLEM DEFINITION

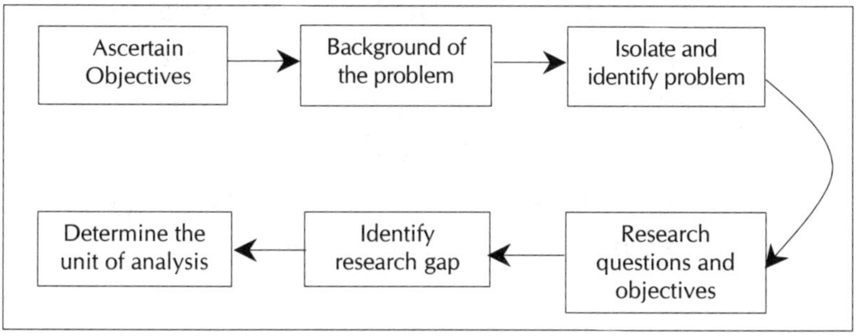

Source: Derived from Zikmund (1999)

The problem definition assisted the design of the research and research master plan. The latter comprises:

1. Data collection methods
2. Sources for information, and
3. Procedures for data analysis.

3.3 EXPLORATORY RESEARCH

3.3.1 CATEGORIES OF EXPLORATORY RESEARCH METHODS

There are four basic categories of exploratory research methods (Zikmund 1999):

1. Experience survey, carried out with knowledgeable persons. This method tends to be informal in general and is useful more for helping to formulate the problem and clarify concepts rather than develop conclusive evidence
2. Secondary data analysis reviews related to literature in the field or similar research

3. Case Studies for obtaining information from one or a few situations that are similar to the researcher's research problem, and
4. Pilot studies which refer to small-scale exploratory research techniques that use sampling for the purpose in general. This includes focus group interviews, projective techniques and in-depth interviews.

This research has been based on one country, Malaysia. As such, it is a case study involving a number of exploratory research techniques to examine the underlying issues.

In this research, an exploratory survey was carried out to identify the problem areas. Secondary data were also obtained to find out how the crisis affected the economy as a whole. Although the research is a case study of a particular country, some aspects of case study methodology are not suitable in this research because the crisis is unique and the response of the government is not common practice with other countries.

The chosen techniques were influenced by the objectives of the research and the nature of the research propositions. Certain factors needed to be taken into consideration such as the Official Secrets Act, and the nature of business corporations in Malaysia, where companies usually preferred to keep their inside-information confidential.

3.3.2 Data Collection Technique

3.3.2.1 Focus Group Interview

The focus group interview allows the researcher to find out the consensus on a given topic. Normally, a selected group of individuals is recruited and the individuals are asked for their perspectives on the related topics. This technique helps the researcher to determine the respondents' attitudes, feelings, beliefs, experience and expectation. Furthermore, the researcher is able to gain much information in a relatively short period of time (Zikmund 1999).

3.3.2.2 Projective Techniques

This is an indirect means of questioning that enables a respondent to "project" beliefs and feelings on a third party, an inanimate object or a task situation. Individuals are expected to interpret the situation in their own words based on their experiences, attitudes, and personality and to express their opinions that may be hidden from others (Zikmund 1999).

3.3.2.3 In-depth Interview

This is a relatively unstructured interview. For this technique, the interviewing skill of the researcher is very important. The researcher has to ensure that the respondents feel free to deliver their ideas, answers or expression without bias and without influencing the direction of the conversation (Zikmund 1999).

3.3.2.4 Sample Survey

A sample survey is a tool to collect primary data from a representative sample of a targeted population. Though most sample survey methods are used for descriptive research, it can also be used for exploratory research and causal research. Under this research technique, three major methods of sampling are commonly used:

1. "Random sampling". A sampling method that can be used by the researcher to select in a way that gives every member of the population an equal chance of being included (Zikmund 1999)
2. "Stratified sampling". The selection of a sample, which can be mathematically representative with regard to significant characteristics. It can be used when particular characteristics of the population are already known (Zikmund 1999), and
3. "Purposive sampling". The selection of a group that is typical of the population as a whole. Data from this method are suitable for indicating conclusions, but not suitable for statistical testing procedures (Zikmund 1999).

3.4 SELECTED TECHNIQUE

3.4.1 DATA COLLECTION TECHNIQUES

The nature of the research proposition and the objectives of the research influence the choice of technique. In order to find out whether companies are affected by currency controls, the profit level and financial standing of the company are required information. However, companies often do not like to share this information. Besides this, subject to Official Secret Act, certain sensitive information cannot be easily obtained.

Taking full account of all these factors, a sample survey, focus group discussion and in-depth interviews were adopted as the principle data collection techniques.

In the process, questions were structured according to the findings from the literature review. As shown in Table 2.3 in the previous chapter, questionnaires and research questions were prepared according to the research gaps that had been identified.

Then, the questionnaires were handed over to a group of knowledgeable persons (Table 3.1) as part of a pilot survey. The questionnaires were readjusted on the basis of their comments.

TABLE 3.1: PILOT SURVEY PARTICIPANTS

Name	Profession/position
Lee Kim Biang	Senior Economist
Tan Koay Lye	Senior Bank Consultant
Goh Joon Hai	Chartered Accountant
Lee Leok Soon	Senior Officer in Malaysian Institute of Corporate Governance

Source: Developed for this research

Focus group discussion was carried out as well. Topics that were to be discussed during the meetings were based on the outlined research proposition (Table 3.2), and the details of the conduct of the focus group discussion are described in Section 3.4.5.

TABLE 3.2: THE FOCUS GROUPS AND TOPICS

Group No.	Focus group	No of Participants	Discussion Topics
1	1 (government institution) 1 (professional body) 3 (higher learning institutions)	5	Research Proposition 1
2	5 (higher learning institutions)	5	Research Proposition 2
3	1 (government institution) 1 (professional body) 3 (higher learning institutions)	5	Research Proposition 3
4	1 (professional body) 4 (higher learning institutions)	5	Research Proposition 4
5	2 (professional bodies) 3 (higher learning institutions)	5	Research Proposition 5

Source: Developed for this research

3.4.2 SECONDARY DATA

Secondary data are the data previously collected for other purposes. The advantage of using secondary data in this analysis is that the data allows analysis/research built on past research. In this analysis, the researcher began with data collection, consisting mainly of information and data from the country's Economic Reports and the Statistics Department Malaysia. From this point, the data was converted from the original form to a format suitable for the research. The data obtained were mainly external sources of data.

Secondary data in this research were needed to pinpoint the differences and performances before and after the imposition of the exchange controls. Focus is directed on the GDP growth, sectoral performances, domestic fronts, balance of payments and government's policies and restructuring process. The data also revealed the response and movements of the government towards the crisis, as well as provided information on the details of the imposed controls in 1998.

3.4.3 SURVEY SAMPLE

Roscoe (1975) has suggested that sample sizes larger than thirty and less than five hundred are appropriate for research. In this research, about 100 entrepreneurs or CEO's or the chairmen of companies were selected from each of the first board and second board-listed companies to answer the questionnaires. Following this, 30 of them, who have been severely affected by the crisis were selected for in-depth interview. The interviewees were not selected based on probability sampling design.

3.4.3.1 THE QUESTIONNAIRE

The survey questionnaire involved structured questions. The questionnaire was structured based on the areas related to the research propositions.

To ensure retention of the respondents' interest and to elicit precise responses, the questions were designed to be simple and mostly closed-ended.

A questionnaire has inherent problems associated with interpretation. A pilot study had been carried out before the questionnaire was sent to the respondents to pre-empt misinterpretation as far as possible. As listed in Table 3.1, four knowledgeable persons were handed the questionnaire and the questions were adjusted and refined on the basis of their comments.

Questions were sent to 200 public-listed companies in Malaysia. The details are set out in Chapter 4.

3.4.4 CONDUCT OF THE FOCUS GROUP DISCUSSIONS

Calls were made on the Chief Executive Officers of the selected case study firms to explain the purpose of the research and to solicit their support and cooperation.

"Discussion guides" were attached to the consent statement to inform them about:

- the purpose of the focus group meeting
- the composition of the group, and
- suggested discussion topics.

The researcher acted as moderator of the focus group meetings which usually comprised of five persons. At the outset, the moderator developed close rapport with each member to promote interaction among the members. Participants were encouraged to speak candidly on the discussion topics and the research proposition and to express their in-depth views. The whole process was unstructured, free-flowing and arranged so that the members and salient issues could easily be identified.

3.4.5 The Focus Groups: Discussion Topics

The research propositions and the topics discussed are outlined below:

- **RESEARCH PROPOSITION 1**
  The currency and capital controls are necessary to insulate the Malaysian economy from the shortcomings of the global financial architecture
- **RESEARCH PROPOSITION 2**
  The capital and currency controls are innovative and appropriate to address the problems of unfettered global currency flows
- **RESEARCH PROPOSITION 3**
  The Malaysian capital and currency controls have contributed to increased foreign and domestic investments
- **RESEARCH PROPOSITION 4**
  The Malaysian capital and currency controls have resulted in speedy economic recovery in the country, and
- **RESEARCH PROPOSITION 5**
  The Malaysian capital and currency controls will enhance the country's global competitive advantage.

As shown in Table 3.2, participants were invited to discuss topics relevant to propositions. Though many topics were discussed in the focus group discussions, they were directed to answer the questions as set out in the questionnaire.

3.5 DATA ANALYSIS PROCEDURES

The data analysis procedures were finalised during the research design planning stage. Given the objectives and the nature of the research, it was deemed necessary to categorise, tabulate and recombine the collected data in a form suitable for testing the research proposition. This required the conduct of statistical analysis with the use of a software system to determine frequency tables, standard deviations and the cross tabulation of the results by groups. The aim was to ascertain the correlation between the survey groups and the emergent patterns as a basis for deriving conclusions and formulating recommendations. The process started with the identification of the key concepts underpinning the research propositions. Each concept was then given an "operational definition" in order to specify the activities necessary to measure them.

The operational definitions were useful for measuring the responses from the experience survey and the focus groups. As these were largely "attitude" responses, attitude rating scales were required. Three scales were considered :

- **SIMPLE ATTITUDE SCALES**

  Respondents were required to either agree or disagree to a question. The scales did not provide for the fine distinctions in the attitudes of the respondents.

- **CATEGORY SCALES**
  This was a more sensitive measure since it provided flexibility for the respondents to choose several response categories
- **THE LIKERT SCALE**
  This summated rating method permitted respondents to select one of five in a range of attitudes, with scores assigned to the alternative responses (Zikmund, 1999). All these scales were used in the questionnaire as appropriate.

In consideration of the complexity and the nature of the questions, a category scale was chosen as the rating scales for the survey.

3.6 RELIABILITY AND VALIDITY

Reliability applies to a measure when similar results are obtained over time and across situations. Reliability can be defined as the degree to which measures are free from error and therefore yield consistent results (Zikmund 1999).

Validity is defined as the ability of a scale or measuring instrument to measure what is intended to be measured. Although reliability is necessary for validity, it is not in itself sufficient (Zikmund 1999).

In this research, both focus group discussions and a survey were carried out. Thus, reliability and validity were achieved. The two techniques of measurement provided good comparison.

3.7 Ethical Issues

The researcher respected the rights of, and met the obligations pertaining to, the other parties, namely, the respondents and Southern Cross University. These included the respondents' rights to privacy and the right to be informed on all aspects of the research.

All the respondents were informed about the nature and purpose of the research. It was verbally agreed that the names of the participants and their organisations would be kept confidential if they so requested. Further, each participant had a choice as to whether to be involved or not.

The researcher on his part maintained objectivity, presented the true research findings and met the requirements of Southern Cross University.

3.8 Conclusion

The design of the research was based on exploratory research and guided by the body of knowledge on research methods. Data was collected through questionnaires, focus group discussion and in-depth interview. Meaningful insight on the research problem was gathered from government policy-makers and industrialists. The result of the primary data collection is presented in Chapter 4 and the results of the secondary data analysis are set out in Section 2.10 and 2.11.

PRIMARY DATA ANALYSIS — THE IMPACT OF THE CONTROLS AND SOME OF ITS CORRELATES

4.1 THE SURVEY

The study aims to look at the impact of the foreign exchange and capital controls on foreign and domestic investments. To this end, a survey was conducted on selected public-listed companies on the Kuala Lumpur Stock Exchange (KLSE). Two hundred companies were selected from different industries, one hundred each from both the main board and the second board of the KLSE.

A questionnaire of 12 questions was mailed to the selected companies. Most of the questions were close-ended with dichotomous or nominal responses. Only three required ordinal answers. The purpose of the questionnaire was to elicit an answer to two research questions:

1. What is the impact of the controls on foreign investment flow and domestic investments?
2. Is there a correlation between the controls and the Malaysian economic recovery underway?

Data collected from the survey was analysed using the Statistical Package for Social Sciences (SPSS).

Section 4.2 gives the background of the responding companies in the survey. Following this, Section 4.3 examines the responses on the impact of the foreign exchange control. Section 4.4 is devoted to examine the respondents' points of view on the capital controls while Section 4.5 examines their perceptions of the ringgit value. A summary of the respondents' perceptions on the economic recovery process is in Section 4.6. Section 4.7 concludes with the implications and recommendations based on the survey.

4.2 Background of the Responding Companies

The mail survey achieved a response rate of 25%, with a total of 50 companies responding. Of these, 52% (26 companies) were companies listed on the main board of the KLSE while the other 48% were companies listed on the second board.

Table 4.1, Figures 4.1 and 4.2 display the industrial background of the companies by board on the KLSE. Most of the responses were collected from companies dealing in industrial products and listed on both the main board and the second board. 27 and 38% of the total responses were from main board and second board listed companies respectively. A similar number of responses was received from trading and services companies on the second board while only 12% of responses were collected from companies listed on the main board in the same category. Only 23 and 13% of the responding companies on the main board and the second board respectively were consumer products companies. No response was received from companies in the finance, properties and mining industries on the second board, just as none was received from companies in the construction industry on the main board. Nineteen percent of the responses on the main board were from the finance sector while 8% were received from the plantation sector companies on the same board. Only one company (4%) each from the properties and plantation sectors from the second board responded to the survey. Similar findings (one company each) were observed from companies from the technology, properties and mining sectors from the main board.

TABLE 4.1 THE INDUSTRIAL BACKGROUND OF COMPANIES BY BOARD ON THE KLSE

	Main Board (%)	Second Board (%)	Total (%)
Consumer Products	23 (6)	13 (3)	18 (9)
Industrial Products	27 (7)	38 (9)	32 (16)
Construction	—	4 (1)	2 (1)
Trading/ Service	12 (3)	38 (9)	24 (12)
Technology	4 (1)	—	2 (1)
Finance	19 (5)	—	10 (5)
Properties	4 (1)	4 (1)	4 (2)
Plantation	8 (2)	4 (1)	6 (3)
Mining	4 (1)	—	2 (1)
Total	100 (26)	100 (24)	100 (50)

Note: Figures in parenthesis refer to number of counts.
Source: Developed from primary data

FIGURE 4.1: THE INDUSTRIAL BACKGROUND OF MAIN BOARD COMPANIES

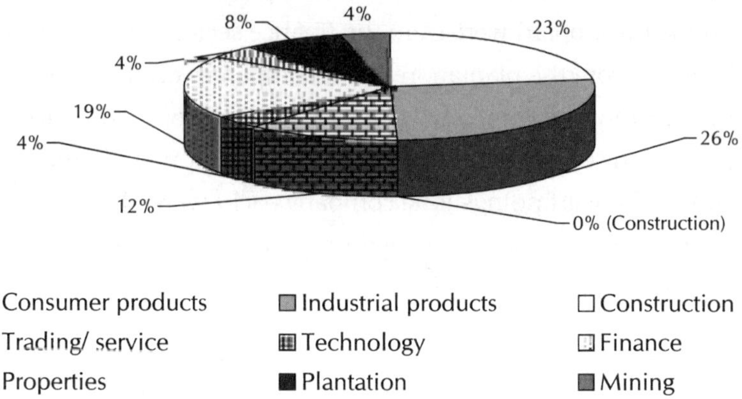

Source: Developed from primary data

FIGURE 4.2: THE INDUSTRIAL BACKGROUND OF SECOND BOARD COMPANIES

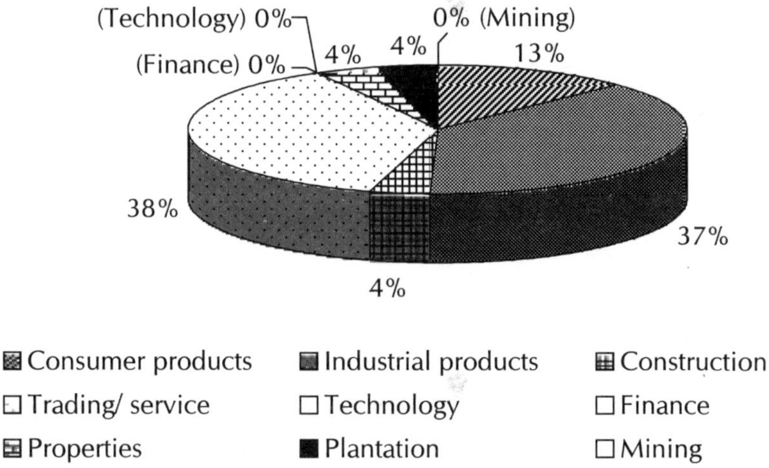

Source: Developed from primary data

4.3 Impact of the Foreign Exchange Control

Three questions were asked in the questionnaire to answer the third research question of the study: *What is the impact of the controls on foreign investment flow and domestic investments?* The questions were:

- **Q1:** Do the existing foreign exchange controls matter to your company?
- **Q2:** Which business activity/activities has/have been affected by the foreign exchange controls: (a) business volume, (b) cash flow (c) financing (d) competitiveness in the domestic/foreign market?
- **Q3:** How has/have the following activity/activities been affected? Are they better or worse: (a) business volume (b) cash flow (c) financing (d) competitiveness in the domestic/foreign market?

Table 4.2 presents responses to these questions. Slightly more than four-fifths (82%) of the respondents reported that the existing foreign exchange controls mattered to their companies, with 77 and 87% from the main board and the second board respectively. The findings showed that other than the response from the construction, technology and mining industries (which were represented by only 1 company responding to the survey) all respondents confirmed that the foreign exchange control had an impact on their business. All the finance companies responding to the survey, and 93% (14 out of 15) of industrial products companies also gave a similar response. Among consumer products companies however, only 78% indicated that the control policies mattered to their companies while one-third (4 out of 12) of the trading/services companies reported that the existing foreign currency control did not matter to their companies.

TABLE 4.2: THE EFFECTS OF FOREIGN CURRENCY CONTROL ON THE RESPONDENT COMPANIES

	Q1	Q2a	Q2b	Q2c	Q2d	Q3a	Q3b	Q3c	Q3d
Main Board (N=26)	77	46	81	85	39	53	63	57	63
Second Board (N=24)	83	63	67	63	42	77	58	54	71
Manufacturing	88 (25)	38 (26)	23 (26)	23 (26)	77 (26)	64 (26)	64 (26)	45 (26)	67 (26)
Non-Manufacturing	75 (24)	54 (24)	29 (24)	29 (24)	42 (24)	64 (24)	56 (24)	67 (24)	67 (24)
Consumer Products	78 (9)	33 (9)	33 (9)	11 (9)	56 (9)	60 (5)	50 (4)	50 (2)	60 (5)
Industrial Products	93 (15)	44 (16)	19 (16)	31 (16)	87 (16)	67 (9)	71 (7)	44 (9)	67 (15)
Construction	100 (1)	0 (1)	0 (1)	100 (1)	0 (1)	—	—	100 (1)	—
Trading/Services	67 (12)	42 (12)	33 (12)	25 (12)	33 (12)	67 (6)	40 (5)	60 (5)	60 (5)
Technology	100 (1)	0 (1)	0 (1)	0 (1)	100 (1)	—	—	—	100 (1)
Finance	100 (5)	100 (5)	20 (5)	20 (5)	60 (5)	40 (5)	100 (1)	100 (1)	33 (3)
Properties	50 (2)	50 (2)	50 (2)	50 (2)	0 (2)	100 (1)	100 (1)	100 (1)	1
Plantations	67 (3)	33 (3)	33 (3)	33 (3)	67 (3)	100 (1)	50 (2)	0 (1)	100 (3)
Mining	100 (1)	100 (1)	0 (1)	0 (1)	100 (1)	100 (1)	—	—	100 (1)
Total (N)	82 (49)	46 (50)	26 (50)	26 (50)	60 (50)	64 (28)	60 (20)	55 (20)	67 (33)

Note: Figures denote proportion of responses of 'Yes' to the questions Q1 and Q2 and 'Better' to question Q3. Numbers in parenthesis refer to the total number of valid cases in that category.

The responding companies were grouped into manufacturing and non-manufacturing industries and it was noted that 52% (26 out of 50) of the responding companies were manufacturing companies with 9 and 16 companies from consumer and industrial products industries respectively, and one from the technology industry.

The findings of the survey showed that 88% of the responding manufacturing companies indicated that the control policies mattered to their companies while only 75% of the non-manufacturing responding companies reported the same. The survey findings appear to support a report by a roundtable interview conducted by a local press, *The Star*, which indicated that 'local manufacturers favour a fixed ringgit rate' (*The Star*, 2 May 2001).

On the other hand, slightly less than half (46%) the respondents indicated in the survey that the business volume of their companies was affected by the foreign exchange control policy, with 54 and 38% from the main board and the second board respectively. All the participating financial institutions reported that their business volumes was affected by the foreign exchange control while the construction and technology industries (N=1 for both industries) indicated that their business volumes was not affected by the policy. Only one-third of the consumer products and plantations companies reported that the business volume of their companies was affected by the policy.

Of the responding manufacturing companies, 38% reported that the business volume of their companies was affected by the foreign exchange control policy but while 54% of the responding non-manufacturing companies responded similarly.

A lower proportion of companies reported that the cash flow of the company was affected by the foreign exchange control policy implemented by the government. Only slightly more than a quarter (26%) of the responding companies reported so. One-third of responses each from the consumer products (3 out of 9), trading and services (4 out of 12) and plantation (1 out of 3) industries also reported that they were similarly affected. About one-fifth (5 out of 26) and one-third (8 out of 24) of companies from the main board and the second board respectively reported that the cash flow of their companies was affected by the foreign exchange control policy.

Only 23 and 29% of the responding manufacturing and non-manufacturing companies reported that the cash flow and financing of their companies was affected by the foreign exchange control policy. The findings seemed to indicate that the majority of the responding companies was not affected.

Similar findings were noted in the impact of the foreign exchange control on the financing of the responding companies. However, a higher proportion (38%) of respondents from the second board reported that the financing of the company was affected by the foreign exchange control policy while only 15% from the main board reported the same. Chi-square analysis showed that the financing of companies listed on the second board was significantly more likely to be affected by the foreign exchange control policy than companies listed on the main board (χ^2 value = 3.172, p-value = 0.075, N = 50).

In the case of whether the competitiveness of the companies in the domestic or foreign market had been affected by the foreign exchange control, 60% of the companies indicated positive. Sixty-two percent of these are listed on the main board and 58% on the second. Most of the companies in the industrial products (87%), plantation (67%), finance (60%) and consumer products (56%) industries reported that the foreign exchange control policy affected their competitiveness. Technology and mining companies reported similar outcomes (both industries with N=1).

TABLE 4.3: THE EFFECT OF CAPITAL CONTROL POLICY ON OVERSEAS INVESTMENTS OF THE RESPONDENT COMPANIES

	Q4
Main Board (N=25)	16
Second Board (N=22)	41
Manufacturing Firms	33 (24)
Non-Manufacturing Firms	22 (23)
Consumer Products	38 (8)
Industrial Products	33 (15)
Construction	0 (1)
Trading/ Services	17 (12)
Technology	0 (1)
Finance	20 (5)
Properties	100 (1)
Plantations	0 (3)
Mining	100 (1)
Total (N)	28 (47)

Note: Figures denote proportion of responses to 'Yes' to the questions Q4. Numbers in parenthesis refer to the total number of valid cases in that category.

On the other hand, contrasting findings were noted when the researcher categorised the responding companies into manufacturing and non-manufacturing sectors. The findings showed that 77% of the manufacturing companies indicated that the competitiveness of their companies in the domestic and foreign market was affected by the implementation of the foreign exchange control policy while only 42% of the responding non-manufacturing companies reported the same. This could be because manufacturers in Malaysia still rely heavily on foreign exchange rates for the import of raw materials or the exports of their finished products. As indicated by the Vice-President of the Federation of Malaysian Manufacturers, Dato' Paul Low, "What we (manufacturers) want is a stable currency irrespective of the level ..." (*The Star*, 2 May 2001). The non-manufacturing sector, such as trading or services however were not much affected by the foreign exchange rates except when they were dealing in imported goods or products.

Forty-six percent of the responding companies reported that the business volume of their companies was affected by the foreign exchange control, with an additional 10% of them mentioning that the business volume had become better or worse as a result. Of the 56% of the companies who responded to the third question: 'How has/have the activity/activities mentioned been affected? Are they better or worse?' 64% (18 out of 28 companies) reported that their business volume had improved while the other 36% reported that the business volume had worsened after the implementation of the policy. Twenty-eight of these companies, 53 and 77% from the main board and the second board respectively, reported that their business volume had improved. Among the industrial products and trading/services companies, two-thirds reported that the business volume of their companies had improved after the implementation of the policy. A similar response was indicated by responding consumer products (60%) and finance (40%). Construction and technology companies did not respond to this question while properties, plantations and mining companies indicated that they have benefited from the implementation of the policy.

A total of 20 companies (40% of the total responding companies) reported that the cash flow of their companies was affected by the foreign exchange control policy. 60% (12 companies) indicated the control had a positive impact on their cash flow while the other 8 companies reported that the control had impacted their cash flow negatively. Sixty percent (12 out of 20 companies) of the companies responding to this question were from the second board. Only 50% of the consumer products and plantations companies and 40% of the trading and services companies reported that the foreign exchange control had a positive impact on the cash flow of their companies. Five out of seven (71%) of industrial products companies reported better cash flow after the control was implemented. Only one company each from the finance and properties industries responded to this question and both indicated a positive impact on their cash flow. Construction, technology and mining companies did not respond to this question.

Twenty companies responded to the question on the aspect of financing. Only 11 companies (55%) indicated that the control policy had a positive effect on the financing of the company. Trading and services (60%), consumer products (50%) and industrial products (44%) companies indicated that the foreign exchange control had improved the financing of their companies. One plantation company indicated that the policy had worsened its financing.

Sixty-six percent (33 out of 50) of the companies responded to the question on competitiveness. Two-thirds of these (33 companies) indicated that the foreign exchange control policy had made them more competitive in the domestic or foreign market. Industrial products (67%), consumer products and trading and services (60% each) companies reported that the implementation of the policy had increased the competitiveness of their products or services. However, only one out of the three finance companies reported the same effect. Slightly more than half (17 out of 33) of the responding companies were from the second board.

Overall, more manufacturing companies reported that the foreign exchange control policy had a positive impact on their cash flow (64%) and competitiveness in the domestic and foreign markets (67%) as compared to non-manufacturing companies. On the other hand, only 45% of responding manufacturers reported that the financing of their companies had become better after the implementation of the foreign exchange control policy while 67% of the responding non-manufacturers reported so.

4.4 Impacts of the Capital Control

The Central Bank of Malaysia announced the implementation of the capital control on 1 September 1998 whereby foreign investors in the Kuala Lumpur Stock Exchange could only repatriate investment from the country free of tax after 1 year from the date of investment. Alternatively, it would be subjected to 10% tax. Although the policy was relaxed in February, and

September 1999 and October 2000, the capital control policy was regarded as a hindrance to foreign funding investing in the KLSE. However, this control policy was removed unexpectedly on 2 May 2001.

In this study, the researcher was also interested in looking at the impact of the capital control on industries, as well as investigating the desired duration for the implementation of the control. Two questions were asked:

- **Q4:** Did the imposed capital control affect your company's investment policy in overseas?
- **Q8:** How long would you like the capital controls to continue?

Only 26% of the respondent companies indicated that the company's investment policy overseas was affected by the capital control policy implemented by the government. About 70% (9 out of 13) of them were from the second board (Table 4.4). Chi-square analysis showed that companies listed on the second board were significantly more likely to be affected by the capital control policy than companies listed on the main board (χ^2 value = 4.7, p-value = 0.096, N = 47).

The results of the study also showed that consumers and industrial products industries were more likely to be affected by the capital control policy than other industries participating in the study. Thirty-eight and 33% of the responding companies respectively reported this. Companies from the constructions, technology and plantations industries reported that their investment policies overseas were not affected by the capital control policy.

TABLE 4.4: THE DESIRED DURATION OF THE CAPITAL CONTROLS

	5 years or more	Less than 5 years	Others
Main Board		79 (24)	21 (24)
Second Board	9 (23)	70 (23)	22 (23)
Manufacturing Firms	4 (24)	79 (24)	17 (24)
Non-Manufacturing Firms	4 (23)	70 (23)	26 (23)
Consumer Products		88 (8)	13 (8)
Industrial Products	7 (15)	80 (15)	13 (15)
Construction		100 (1)	
Trading/ Services	9 (11)	64 (11)	27 (11)
Technology			100 (1)
Finance		60 (5)	40 (5)
Properties		50 (2)	50 (2)
Plantations		100 (1)	
Mining		100 (1)	
Total (N)	4 (47)	75 (47)	21 (47)

Figures in parenthesis indicate the number of valid cases.

Thirty-three percent of the responding manufacturing companies indicated that the imposed capital control had affected their companies' investment policy overseas while only 22% of the non-manufacturing companies reported so. Again, the findings revealed that the capital control policy implemented by the government affected manufacturing companies more than non-manufacturing companies.

On the question of how long the respondents would like the capital control policy to continue, 90% of them indicated that it should not exceed 5 years, while 20% preferred the policy to be lifted by 2002 (2 years from the time the survey was conducted in 2000). Only two companies from the second board preferred the capital control to continue for more than 10 years or between 5 and 10 years (1 company each). Twenty percent of the respondents (10 companies) indicated 'Other' as the preferred duration for the capital control policy to continue (Table 4.4) and further analysis showed that the preferred duration ranged between ½ and 2 years.

No difference was seen in the response of manufacturing and non-manufacturing companies to the question on the preferred duration of the capital control policy. Most of them indicated that they preferred the control to be removed before 2005.

4.5 Perceptions of Respondents on the Ringgit Value

Responses were also collected on the peg value of ringgit. Currently, the ringgit Malaysia (RM) value remains at 1 September 1998 pegged value of RM3.80 to a US dollar. The three questions asked were:

- **Q5:** Has your company committed to foreign currency borrowings?
- **Q6:** Do you think that Malaysia ringgit (RM) is undervalued at the current rate?

- **Q7:** Ringgit is currently fixed at RM3.80=US$1. What range do you think would be the best peg for the ringgit?

Only 14% (7 out of 49 companies) reported that they were committed to foreign currency borrowings. Seventy-one percent (5 out of 7) of these companies were listed on the main board. Nineteen percent (3 out of 16) and 11% (1 out of 9) of the industrial and consumer products companies respectively indicated that they had foreign currency borrowings. The other companies committed to foreign currency borrowings were from trading and services, finance and property industries (1 company each). Only 15 and 13% of the manufacturing and non-manufacturing responding companies respectively indicated that they had committed to foreign borrowings.

In response to the question whether ringgit Malaysia was undervalued, 90% of the responding companies indicated in the affirmative. Only 6% reported that RM was not undervalued and 4% of them had no opinion on the issue. This was one of the few questions that received a similar response from the responding companies regardless of their industrial background and their board listing.

On the other hand, all the responding non-manufacturers indicated that the ringgit was undervalued while 14% of the responding manufacturers did not think so. The Vice-President of the Federation of Malaysian Manufacturers, Dato' Paul Low believes that it is because having a fixed rate enables easier negotiation of prices for manufacturers. It is thus preferable to the slight change in profit margin that might be attained if the ringgit value was subjected to change regularly. As reported in *The Star*:

TABLE 4.5: THE PERCEPTION ON RINGGIT VALUE BY THE RESPONDENT COMPANIES

	Q5	Q6
Main Board (N = 26)	19	92
Second Board (N = 24)	9	87
Manufacturing Firms	15 (26)	86 (22)
Non-manufacturing Firms	13 (23)	100 (23)
Consumer Products	11 (9)	88 (8)
Industrial Products	19 (16)	86 (14)
Construction	0 (1)	100 (1)
Trading/Services	9 (11)	100 (11)
Technology	0 (1)	—
Finance	20 (5)	100 (5)
Properties	50 (2)	100 (2)
Plantations	0 (3)	100 (3)
Mining	0 (1)	100 (1)
Total (N)	14 (49)	93 (45)

Note: Figures denote proportion of responses to 'Yes' to questions Q5 and Q6. Figures in parenthesis indicate the total number of valid cases.

"… He sees that the weaker ringgit would provide a higher profit. In many cases, we (the manufacturers) are weak in our marketing and this puts us in a weak bargaining position … " (*The*

Star, 2 May 2001) In the same report, Dato' Low also mentioned that "... The peg should not be changed just because of temporary events ... " (*The Star*, 2 May 2001)

TABLE 4.6: THE PREFERRED PEG VALUE FOR RINGGIT TO ONE US DOLLAR

	4.00-4.50	3.50-4.00	3.00-3.50	2.50-3.00	Others
Manufacturing Firms	4 (24)	29 (24)	58 (24)	4 (24)	4 (24)
Non-Manufacturing Firms	—	9 (22)	86 (22)	5 (22)	—
Consumer Products	—	25 (8)	75 (8)	—	—
Industrial Products	7 (15)	33 (15)	53 (15)	7 (15)	—
Construction	—	—	100 (1)	—	—
Trading/Services	—	10 (10)	80 (10)	10 (10)	—
Technology	—	—	—	—	100 (1)
Finance	—	20 (5)	80 (5)	—	—
Properties	—	—	100 (2)	—	—
Plantations	—	—	100 (3)	—	—
Mining	—	—	100 (1)	—	—
Total (N)	2 (46)	20 (46)	72 (46)	4 (46)	2 (46)

Note: Figures denote proportion of responses to 'Yes' to questions Q5 and Q6. Figures in parenthesis indicate the total number of valid cases.

Seventy-two percent of the respondent companies expressed the view that the peg should be set at "RM3.00 – RM3.50" per US dollar while 20% indicated that the peg rate should be set between RM3.50 – RM4.00. Four percent, one each from the industrial products, and trading and services industries (both companies from the second board) preferred the peg rate to be in the range of RM2.50 – RM3.00. One responding company indicated that the current rate (RM3.80 = US$1) was the best peg value.

Differences were again seen in the responses between manufacturing and non-manufacturing companies with regard to the peg value of the ringgit. One-third (8 out of 24) of the manufacturing companies indicated that the peg value of the ringgit should be set above RM3.50 to a US dollar while only 9% (2 out 22) of the non-manufacturing companies concurred. The findings appear to indicate that compared to the non-manufacturers, more manufacturers tended to prefer a more stable exchange rate for the ease of negotiation as mentioned by the vice-president of FMM. Twenty-nine percent of the responding manufacturing companies felt that the best rate should be between RM3.50 and RM4.00 to a US dollar while 4% (1 company) indicated that RM3.80 was the best rate.

4.6 PERCEPTIONS OF RESPONDENTS ON THE ECONOMIC RECOVERY

In order to understand whether there was a correlation between the economic recovery in the country and the controls policy, the researcher also included the following four questions:

- **Q9:** Although the Malaysian government has officially declared that the recession is over. Has your company also recovered?

- **Q10:** Notwithstanding Q9, how would you describe your attitude towards the economic recovery in Malaysia?
- **Q11:** Do you think that the Malaysian economic recovery is due to the imposed foreign exchange controls?
- **Q12:** Do you think that the Malaysian economic recovery is due to the imposed capital controls?

Tables 4.7 and 4.8 present the responses to these questions by the participating companies. Table 4.7 shows that about 90% of the responding companies listed on both the main board and the second board indicated that their companies had recovered from the economic recession since 1997. This was reflected in all the industries except for the plantation companies, with only 33% in agreement. More manufacturing (92%) than non-manufacturing responding companies (83%) indicated that their companies had recovered from the economic recession.

Table 4.8 presents the respondents' attitudes towards the economic recovery in Malaysia. Most of them were optimistic while 6% were neutral. These companies were from the consumer products and industrial products industries. About 70% of the respondents (70 and 80% from the main board and the second board respectively) felt fairly optimistic about the economic recovery in the country. Non-manufacturing companies appeared more optimistic than the manufacturing ones.

Table 4.7 also shows that about 78% of the responding companies, 73 and 83% respectively from the main board and the second board, felt that the fast economic recovery achieved in the country was due to the currency control policy implemented by the

TABLE 4.7: THE PERCEPTIONS ON THE ECONOMIC RECOVERY IN THE COUNTRY

	Q9	Q11	Q12
Main Board	89 (N=26)	73 (N=26)	54 (N=24)
Second Board	88 (N=23)	83 (N=23)	52 (N=21)
Manufacturing Firms	92 (25)	77 (2)	50 (24)
Non-manufacturing Firms	83 (24)	78 (23)	57 (21)
Consumer Products	100 (9)	78 (9)	50 (8)
Industrial Products	87 (15)	81 (16)	53 (15)
Construction	100 (1)	100 (1)	100 (1)
Trading/Services	83 (12)	73 (11)	60 (10)
Technology	100 (1)	0 (1)	0 (1)
Finance	100 (5)	60 (5)	60 (5)
Properties	100 (2)	100 (2)	50 (2)
Plantations	33 (3)	100 (3)	0 (3)
Mining	100 (1)	100 (1)	100 (1)
Total (N)	88 (49)	78 (49)	53 (45)

Note: Figures denote proportion of responses to 'Yes' to the questions Q9, Q11 and Q12. Figures in parenthesis indicate the total number of valid cases.

government in 1998. However, 8% (4 out of 49 companies) indicated that the recovery could be due to other reasons such as the strong foreign direct investment that was already in place.

Other respondents saw the economic recovery as generally a regional issue rather than a local one. Another respondent mentioned that the economy recovery was due to government efforts and that the foreign exchange control was just one of them. No difference was seen in the response provided by manufacturing and non-manufacturing companies (78 and 77% respectively) participating in the survey.

TABLE 4.8: ATTITUDE TOWARDS THE ECONOMIC RECOVERY

	Very Optimistic	Fairly Optimistic	Neutral
Main Board	23 (26)	69 (26)	8 (26)
Second Board	17 (24)	79 (24)	4 (24)
Consumer Products	11.1 (9)	66.7 (9)	22.2 (9)
Industrial Products	25.0 (16)	68.8 (16)	6.3 (16)
Construction	—	100.0 (1)	—
Trading/Services	8.3 (12)	91.7 (12)	—
Technology	—	100 (1)	—
Finance	40.0 (5)	60.0 (5)	—
Properties	—	100.0 (2)	—
Plantations	66.7 (3)	33.3 (3)	—
Mining	—	100 (1)	—
Total	20.0 (50)	74.0 (50)	6.0 (50)

Note: Figures denote proportion of responses to Q10.
Figures in parenthesis indicate the total number of valid cases.

Respondents from the finance and technology industries did not associate the success of the economic recovery with the implementation of the foreign exchange control policy by the government while 78 and 81% of the respondents from the consumer products and industrial products sectors respectively thought the foreign exchange control was the reason for the success of the economy recovery.

On the other hand, Table 4.7 also shows that only 54 and 52% of responding companies from the main board and the second board respectively thought that the economic recovery in the country was due to the capital control policy implemented by the government. Forty percent of the total responding companies thought otherwise. Thirteen percent of the responding companies, all from the main board, thought that the economic recovery was the result of other factors such as the global market recovery, foreign exchange control policy and regional economic recovery. The table also shows that only 60% of the responding companies in the finance and trading and services industries agreed that the capital control contributed to the economic recovery while only half of the consumer products, industrial products and properties companies shared the same view. A higher proportion of the non-manufacturers (57%) believed that the country's economic recovery was due to the imposed capital control policy while only half of the manufacturers shared the view.

4.7 Focus Group Perspectives on each Proposition

Each of the research issues was addressed by the groups mentioned in Sections 3.4.4 and 3.4.5. Each of the groups comprised five participants. The results of the group discussions on each proposition are summarised below:

- **RESEARCH PROPOSITION 1:** The currency and capital controls are necessary to insulate the Malaysian economy from the shortcomings of the global financial architecture.

  The research issue was addressed by Group 1, comprising one representative from a government agency, three participants from local universities and one from a professional body.

  The five participants generally agreed that:

1. The currency and capital controls were necessary to control the outflows of funds from the country during a crisis.
2. Capital control should not operate on a long-term basis as it may might affect capital inflows into the country.
3. The export-oriented manufacturing sector had benefited from the currency and capital controls, and.
4. Free flow of capital might create volatility in the exchange market as well as affect the liquidity of a particular nation.

The viewpoints from the groups reinforced the results from both the secondary data analysis and the responses of the survey. Accordingly this study accepts Research Proposition 1, that the currency and capital controls were necessary to insulate the Malaysian economy from the shortcomings of the global financial architecture.

- **RESEARCH PROPOSITION 2:** The capital and currency controls are innovative and appropriate to address the problems of unfettered global currency flow.

  The research issue was raised during the discussion with Group 2. The group comprised five participants, all from local higher educational institutions.

  The participants generally agreed that:

1. Unfettered global currency flow could create a bubble economy, which might lead to a current-account deficit.
2. The financial liberalisation that allows currency flow freely from country to country may create an economic shock, especially to a small economy.
3. The currency and capital controls are important to a small economy such as Malaysia to withstand pressure from the international market during a crisis, and
4. The currency and capital controls were needed to buy time for internal restructuring and to nurture the economy.

The results suggested support for Research Proposition 2, that the capital and currency controls were innovative and appropriate to address the problems of unfettered global currency flow.

- **RESEARCH PROPOSITION 3:** The Malaysian capital and currency controls have contributed to increased foreign and domestic investments.

  To discuss this research issue, five participants, one from a government institution, one from a professional body, and three from local universities were invited.

  It was generally agreed that:

1. The capital and currency controls had not contributed to increased investment both from the domestic and the international markets, and
2. Investors, particularly short-term foreign ones, did not welcome the controls.

Generally, the results above rejected the Research Proposition 3. Together with the results from both secondary data analysis and survey responses, they appeared to confirm that the controls may have negative effects on both the domestic and foreign investment.

- **RESEARCH PROPOSITION 4:** The Malaysian capital and currency controls have resulted in a speedy economic recovery in the country.

  To discuss this research issue, five participants, one from a professional body and four from local universities were invited.

  They generally agreed to the following:

1. The economy would be getting back on track very soon. Despite the slow growth in international

economy since year 2000, the Malaysian economy had benefited from both the exports of both palm oil and crude oil.

2. The exchange controls contributed more to export-led industries, and
3. The controls allowed the government and corporates to undertake economic restructuring more efficiently.

The results seemed to support the Research Proposition 4, that the capital and currency controls have resulted in speedy economic recovery in the country.

- **RESEARCH PROPOSITION 5:** The Malaysian capital and currency controls will enhance the country's global competitive advantage.

The research issue was raised during the discussion with Group 5, comprising three participants from local higher educational institutions of learning and two from professional bodies.

The Group agreed that:

1. The effects of the controls have been played down by the regional currency exchange rates. The pegged rate was seen to be overvalued especially in year 2001, and
2. Malaysian exports were not as competitive as those from other regional countries.

Overall result of the discussion on this Research Proposition rejected Research the Proposition 5., where the results of the group discussion and primary data analysis confirmed that the controls did not enhance the country's global competitive advantage.

4.7.1 Implications and Recommendations

The findings of the survey indicated that the existing foreign exchange control mattered to most of the responding companies. The findings also revealed that the control policy affected competitiveness and business volume more than the cash flow and the financing of these companies. However, a greater number of the companies reported that the business volume, cash flow, financing and competitiveness had improved after the implementation of the control policy. The findings also revealed that the financing of companies listed on the second board was significantly more likely to be affected by the control than companies listed on the main board. This appeared to indicate that overall, the foreign exchange control policy implemented by the government had assisted the industries in coping with the economic recession and financial crisis experienced in 1997. This implied that the foreign exchange control should remain. This was in line with the decision of the Central Bank (Bank Negara) to maintain the foreign exchange control policy in the *Bank Negara Report* 2000/2001 released in April 2001 (*Bank Negara Malaysia* 2001).

The findings also showed that most of the respondents would prefer the capital control policy to be removed after 2005. The findings also showed that the capital control policy was significantly more likely to affect the overseas investment of companies listed on the second board than those listed on the main board. The implication is that the capital control policy restricted the overseas investment of some respondents even though two-thirds of them reported that they were not affected by the policy. However, almost all respondents indicated that the policy should be removed before 2005. This seemed to imply that the capital control policy may not have assisted them in their business, regardless of any restrictions it may have imposed on them.

The findings also indicated that about 90% of the respondents thought that ringgit is undervalued and more than 70% indicated that it should be pegged at RM3.00 to RM3.50 per US dollar. However, financial institutions such as HSBC (Hong Kong and Shanghai Bank Corporation) thought that the ringgit value should be maintained at the current peg despite the slow down in the global economy (*Business Times*, 11 April 2001). A similar view was voiced by the Minister of International Trade and Industry Dato' Seri Rafidah Aziz (*New Straits Times*, 11 April 2001). Policy planners may need to study the impact of re-adjusting the peg value on international competitiveness, balance of payments and its implication on foreign direct investment, in addition to its impact on local consumption and production.

The optimistic attitudes of the respondents toward the economic recovery in the country and the high proportion of them indicating that their companies had recovered from the recession implied that most industries were out of the financial crisis experienced in 1997. However, the global recession experienced by the world economy since late 2000 may have changed this attitude and some industries may be experiencing another recession due to the slowdown of the global market. This is revealed in the adjustment of the forecast of the net growth in

GDP by the Malaysian Institute of Economic Research (MIER) recently.

Most respondents associated the economy recovery to the foreign exchange control policy but fewer associated it to with the capital control policy implemented in the country. The findings seemed to imply that the implementation of the foreign exchange policy by the government had been successful in dealing with the financial crisis experienced in 1997. This was also reflected by manufacturers participating in the research as well as the Vice-President of the Federation of Malaysian Manufacturers in a roundtable discussion with *The Star*. More research should be done in the future to better understand the impact of foreign exchange control policy on the business of industries and the circumstances for it to be effective.

Overall, the research had successfully identified the impacts of the foreign exchange and capital control policies on the business of public-listed companies in the country. Future research may attempt to look at the impact of such policies in an environment of recession in the global market.

CONCLUSION AND IMPLICATIONS

5.1 INTRODUCTION

This research investigated the research problem "What is the impact of exchange controls for sustainable national economic growth?" Commencing with a literature review and secondary data analysis (Chapter 2), it then identified the research gaps. Based on that four research questions were posted.

This chapter is presented in seven sections. Section 5.2 is devoted to the conclusions drawn on each of the propositions, having taken into full account the findings of the literature review and the primary and secondary data analyses.

Following that, Section 5.3 addresses the research problem as deduced from the conclusions in Section 5.2.

Since the research issues are relatively new to policy formulation, Section 5.4 covers the implications for policy and practice.

Section 5.5 addresses the limitations and the constraints that arose during the conduct of the research.

Finally, Section 5.6 concludes with a discussion on the need and opportunities for subsequent study and research.

5.2 Conclusions about each Research Proposition

This section aims at drawing pertinent conclusions about each proposition as a prelude to addressing the research problem in the next section. The propositions in this research are:

- The currency and capital controls are necessary to insulate the Malaysian economy from the shortcomings of the global financial architecture
- The capital and currency controls are innovative and appropriate to address the problems of unfettered global currency flow
- The Malaysian capital and currency controls have contributed to the increased foreign and domestic investments
- The Malaysian capital and currency controls have assisted in speedy economic recovery in the country, and
- The Malaysian capital and currency controls will enhance the country's global competitive advantage.

5.2.1 Research Proposition 1: The currency and capital controls are necessary to insulate the Malaysian economy from the shortcomings of the global financial architecture.

The secondary data analysis (Chapter 2) shows that the currency and capital controls have contributed to the economic recovery. The strong growth of GDP after the imposition of controls is strong evidence of the effectiveness of the controls (Section

2.11.2). In the process of recovery, (Section 2.11.3), the manufacturing sector has benefited most. Domestic demand over the years has improved. Though private investment has declined, the government's expansionary fiscal policy has played a role in boosting aggregate demand. Throughout the analysis, there is no evidence to show that the improved domestic demand is due to the exchange controls.

The inflow of long-term capital into the country is not as strong as it was before the crisis. Though foreign funds are coming in, they are offset by an outflow of foreign funds as soon as the capital controls on foreign funds are relaxed. Current account also registered positive growth after the implementation of the controls, although it has started to decline since the year 2000, as has also the country's international reserves. Should both the trends continue Malaysia would be faced with added challenges. From the facts above, it can be concluded that the capital and currency controls are necessary in the short-run. However, the fact that foreign investments are not coming in is indicative that it affects balance of payments.

The primary data analysis (Chapter 4) indicates that the controls matter to the companies in Malaysia. The survey shows that almost all the respondents want the capital control policy to be removed after 2005. Most businesses in Malaysia do not want the control to be continued in the long-run. Short-term however, these controls appear to have benefited firms in the way they coped with the economic and the financial crises.

In general, both the primary data (Chapter 4) and secondary data (Chapter 2) analyses confirm that Research Proposition 1 is upheld. The currency and capital controls are necessary to insulate the Malaysian economy from the shortcomings of the global financial architecture, at least on a short-term basis.

5.2.2 Research Proposition 2: The capital and currency controls are innovative and appropriate to address the problems of unfettered global currency flow

As noted in the Literature Review (Section 2.3), there are pros and cons to the exchange controls. Capital liberalisation is basically good for a developing economy with a sound financial system because it allows the emerging countries to import capital, technology and hence innovation. However, facts reveal that investment in developing countries can earn higher returns. Massive capital pouring into a developing economy may lead to a bubble economy. It may also lead to a current-account deficit, especially if it is a small country. Therefore, currency controls or capital controls have helped stabilise an economy, as well as to prevent an unwanted crisis or a bubble economy.

Besides Malaysia, many other countries have experienced implementing exchange controls with adjustment to suit their economic standing (Section 2.3.3). The results of the exchange controls depended on the time span of the implementation of the controls, and on the conditions in the domestic and international economies.

The secondary data analysis shows that the overall progress of the economy is an indication that the controls are suitable in the short-run. During the crisis, unfettered currency flow may force a nation to depreciate its currency to an unrealistically low rate. At the same time, the free flow of short-term capital creates a bubble economy, as well as causes panic in the markets, even when the fundamentals of the economy are good.

The currency and capital controls in Malaysia allow the country to re-engineer the domestic economy. The fixed exchange rate enables Bank Negara Malaysia to keep interest rates low, thereby encouraging investment and consumption. The fixed exchange rate also helps export-oriented companies to export their goods and services at a stable price. Capital control in Malaysia enables the country to pre-empt massive capital outflow by removing the pressure to lower the country's international reserves. With these two controls, the government can restructure the domestic economy with low rates of interest without worrying about capital outflow and the depreciation of the exchange rate, both of which may worsen the competitiveness of the country's export goods and services.

The imposition of the controls is similar to buying time for internal restructuring. The controls are appropriate for addressing the problem of unfettered currency flow, which has created unstable circumstances in the economy. If continued, however, the controls would gradually create other problems for the country.

Research Proposition 2 is accepted, backed by both the primary and secondary data analyses. Both capital and currency controls are appropriate to address the problems of unfettered currency flow.

5.2.3 Research Proposition 3: The Malaysian Capital and Currency Controls Have Contributed to Increased Foreign and Domestic Investments.

Primary data indicates that the capital control affects Malaysian firms in their overseas investments, since those affected would have difficulty financing or investing abroad. The capital control therefore does not contribute to Malaysian overseas investment.

The secondary data analysis indicates that both domestic and foreign private investments are declining after the crisis and the imposition of the capital control. There are many factors eroding investors' confidence. The political instability in the South East Asian countries, especially Indonesia, is one factor. There are also issues of corporate governance in Malaysia, especially with regard transparency. A third factor is the poor world economic outlook which has further discouraged investment. Meanwhile, the currency peg of RM3.80 to US$1 in Malaysia may need to be depreciated as the currencies of the countries in the region have further depreciated. Finally, the capital control is not favourable to foreign investors.

It is clear therefore, that the findings of both analyses reject Research Proposition 3. The data show that both domestic and foreign private investments decreased after the imposition of the exchange controls.

5.2.4 Research Proposition 4: The Malaysian capital and currency controls have assisted in speedy economic recovery in the country.

From primary data, respondents were optimistic about the economic recovery and most of them indicated that their companies have recovered from the recession. However, the attitude of the respondents toward the economic recovery might have already shifted considering the change in the state of the global economy since late 2000.

The primary data also indicate that the economic recovery is related more to the foreign exchange policy than capital control policy. The findings seem to imply that exchange control policy has been successful in dealing with the 1997 financial crisis.

Though the secondary data analysis shows no sign of an economic downturn, the forecast of the net growth in Malaysia's GDP for the year 2001 has been readjusted to a lower rate by the MIER.

Both the primary and secondary data seem to indicate that there has been economic recovery in the country. However, two keys for recovery have not been met. The first is structural reforms. The restructuring of financial institutions has not proven effective enough. Inefficient enterprises still remain and have not been allowed to go bankrupt. At the same time, corporate governance, transparency and accounting practices have not improved much. Secondly, investor confidence does not seem to have been restored. There is still capital outflow and many existing foreign investors are closing their branches in Malaysia.

The world economic downturn since late 2000 has blurred the effectiveness of the controls imposed by the Malaysian government. This has made it difficult to do the analysis because some of the improvements in the economy have been offset by the downturn. One is thus left with the question whether the recovery plan, which includes the measures of exchange controls, has been inefficient or whether it is the world economic downturn that has offset the effect of the recovery plan.

Research Proposition 4 – that the Malaysian capital and currency controls have assisted in speedy economic recovery in the country – is supported by the findings in both the primary and secondary data.

5.2.5 RESEARCH PROPOSITION 5: THE MALAYSIAN CAPITAL AND CURRENCY CONTROLS WILL ENHANCE THE COUNTRY'S GLOBAL COMPETITIVE ADVANTAGE.

The findings from the primary data analysis indicate that the ringgit has been undervalued. However, in the year 2001, more currencies in the region have depreciated due to political and financial travails, thus depreciating the relative value of the ringgit in international markets. At the same time, depreciating regional currencies have rendered the current peg of the Malaysian ringgit to US dollar overvalued, thereby affecting the country's global competitive advantage.

It would seem therefore that the role of currency control could be played down by regional developments. Alongside the depreciated regional currencies, falling external demand and the fixed exchange rate are eroding export competitiveness. In order to remain competitive, Malaysian exports must cut prices.

Even when the capital control imposed by the government has been relaxed and in fact is being gradually removed, foreign investors are still not coming in. One reason for this is that foreign investors have lost confidence in the country, while on the other hand, other countries in the region, especially China, are attracting substantial foreign direct investment (FDI) from developed countries. Malaysia is losing her competitive advantage against these countries in competing for FDI.

Research Proposition 5 is therefore rejected based on the analyses. The exchange rate peg is linked to regional exchange rates in determining the competitiveness of the country and the capital control has driven foreign investors away.

The methodology of the research was designed to examine the qualitative and quantitative insight of the research propositions. The sample survey and focus group discussions provided viewpoints for discovering subjective issues in the research. Part of the conclusions of the research propositions was formed from the viewpoints of the research respondents. The responses were examined by using statistical analysis. Besides results from the respondents, the conclusions of Research Propositions 3, 4 and 5 are also the result of economic analysis. BNM, the Ministry of Finance and the Department of Statistics provided strong and valid secondary data which helped crystallise the research issues.

5.3 CONCLUSIONS ABOUT THE RESEARCH PROBLEM

The research problem in this study is: "What is the impact of exchange controls for sustainable national economic growth?" There was a high degree of ambiguity and uncertainty about the problem.

All the findings indicate that exchange controls are needed for sustainable economic growth. Propositions 1, 2 and 4 confirmed several issues. First, exchange controls did help stabilise the Malaysian economy from external uncertainty caused by the shortcomings of the global financial architecture. Second, the controls restricted the free flow of capital, thereby restricting capital outflow. Third, the exchange controls assisted in speedy economic recovery in the country.

By highlighting the impact of exchange controls and the economic performance throughout the years, these findings show that the research problem is relevant. The propositions in the previous section indicate that exchange controls are positively related to economic growth in the short-run. However, the sustainability of the economic growth under exchange controls policy in the long-run has yet to be determined.

In order to have a better understanding of the research problem, exploratory research was conducted. The output of the literature review and the conclusions on the research propositions gave comprehensive and useful insights on the research gaps. They supported the relevance of the research problem (as shown in Table 5.1).

Table 5.2 shows the overall response patterns of the survey on the research propositions.

5.4 IMPLICATIONS FOR POLICY AND PRACTICE

5.4.1 IMPLICATIONS FOR POLICY

The findings of the research have implications for public policy formulation. As exchange controls have been implemented in 1998 and some of the controls have been eliminated, the policy of the government should be focused on how to generate and sustain growth under the existing exchange controls policy in the short-run. In the long run, the government should be considering whether to remove the controls.

Up to the completion of this research (year 2001), the exchange controls have been liberalised. A few of the important rules have been relaxed including:

- Foreign direct investment flow is freely allowed
- Current account transactions are fully convertible
- Credit facilities from domestic banks to non-residents are extended
- Short-term currency swap arrangement is allowed for authorised dealers, and

- Non-residents are allowed to freely repatriate their principal and profits out of the country.

TABLE 5.1: OUTCOMES OF RESEARCH ISSUES

Research Issues	Literature Review Findings	Research Gaps	Literature Review Findings
The need for exchange controls to overcome the shortcomings of the global financial architecture	No	The effectiveness of the Malaysian exchange control policy	Yes
Appropriateness of exchange controls to overcome the problems of currency flow		The appropriateness of exchange control in addressing the problem of unfettered currency flow	
• Global currency flow	Yes		Yes
• Malaysian experience	No		Yes
Impact on foreign and domestic investment	No	Influence of exchange controls on sentiments of both foreign and domestic investors	Yes
Impact on Malaysian economic recovery	No	Suitability of exchange controls to assist Malaysian economic recovery	Yes
Impact on Malaysian global competitive advantage	No	Importance of exchange controls to enhance global competitive advantage	Yes

Source: Developed for the research

TABLE 5.2: OVERALL RESPONSE PATTERNS

Research Proposition	Literature Review	Focus Groups	Survey
1	Unknown	Yes	Yes
2	Unknown	Yes	Yes
3	Unknown	No	No
4	Unknown	Yes	Yes
5	Unknown	No	No

Yes=Concurrence, No=Rejection, Varied=Mixed responses
Source: Developed from the Research Data

These changes are important moves as the global environment has changed. The gradual liberalisation indicates that the government recognises the shortcoming of the controls in the long run.

It is noticed that many developing countries in the region are competing for foreign direct investment. At the same time, foreign investors are keener to invest in a nation with a friendly environment. Capital controls will threaten foreign investors even if the economic fundamentals are sound.

Though the capital control policy has been liberalised, the government needs to pay more attention to sustain investor confidence. One way of doing it is to ensure the consistency of the government in removing the capital control. At the same time, the corporate and economic environment should be restructured.

The imposition of capital and currency controls should buy more time for restructuring the ailing corporate and financial system. Though special purpose vehicles such as Danaharta and Danamodal have been established to restructure ailing corporates and to absorb non-performing loans (NPLs), the government's effort to date has not proven fruitful.

From facts, the government is paying a lot of attention to bailing out government-linked corporates; most of them are not allowed to go bankrupt. The process is not transparent and the level of efficiency is questionable. In the financial system, mergers are encouraged, NPLs have been reduced and steps have been taken to strengthen the financial system. However, the process of bank mergers is slow and efficiency level doubtful. The bonds market is still not well monitored and the equity market is not efficient either.

Up to the completion of the research, the currency control is still being maintained. Ringgit is still pegged to the US dollar at US$1:RM3.8. The fixed exchange rate helps export-oriented companies in terms of price stability. It also eliminates the pressure on the government, as the government tends to maintain low interest rates to nurse the ailing economy. However, in the current development, regional currencies have been depreciated against the US dollar. That has created pressure for the ringgit, as the depreciation of regional currencies has eroded the competitiveness of Malaysian exports.

From the research (literature review), it seems that the fixed exchange rate is beneficial to the economy in the short-term. As a country with an open economic policy, Malaysia would benefit more under a floating exchange rate system.

There are still certain important keys for recovery which have not been met during the implementation of the exchange controls. They are:

- Transparency and accountability of government operations
- Corporate governance
- Trade and financial liberalisation
- Structural reform in the financial sector
- Allowing inefficient enterprises to go bankrupt, and
- Restoring investor confidence.

The government should strengthen all the above before the onset of the next challenge.

5.4.2 IMPLICATION FOR PRACTICE

Though research has confirmed that the exchange and capital controls have assisted the economic recovery, the private sector must not expect the economic prosperity of 1986 to 1997 to repeat in the near future. In fact, the prosperity of Malaysia from 1986 onwards was due to the implementation of the Plaza Accord where the US had forced Japan to appreciate its yen. That has forced Japan to relocate a lot of factories and investments to South East Asian countries, thereby creating a large flow of FDI into these countries. After the Japanese investment, short-term funds followed to join the crowd to boost up the stock market and create immense liquidity in the market.

When the 1997/98 financial crisis hit Malaysia, near-chaos followed. Stabilisation measures were immediately put in place, such as capital and currency controls, the pegging of the ringgit and making it illegal outside Malaysia and the formation of Danaharta and Danamodal. Although these helped the Malaysian private sector in terms of liquidity and the stabilisation of the exchange rate, not all sectors have recovered. Economy recovery is extremely uneven. Only the electronics sector, petroleum and palm oil have managed to do quite well over the past three years. That notwithstanding, the demand for electronic components has decreased.

Electronics forms 60% of our total exports and 21% of our total exports go to the US. Prices for petroleum too have dropped from US$36 to US$26 per barrel. Despite the price drop, Petronas made RM139 billion in 2001. However, companies involved in electronics are mostly foreign-owned. The effects have not filtered down to the general economy. So too with petroleum. Only one company is making the profit. And again the effect has not filtered down into the general economy. The last sector is palm oil. A few plantation companies were making money but now they are trying very hard to break even. The other areas are still very weak and the demand from both domestic and overseas market is relatively lethargic. Meanwhile private sectors continue to face liquidity problems.

Despite relying heavily on the advantage of low exchange rate to obtain competitive advantage, the private sector should improve their product quality. As indicated in the research, exchange controls and/or the pegged ringgit will create more problems in the long run. The private sectors should improve their productivity and product quality when they are still protected by the controls.

5.5 LIMITATIONS

The research process faced some limitations which may affect the conclusions of the propositions.

- The representativeness of the survey sample. Two hundred public-listed companies were selected for the study, thus limiting the generalisability of the results nation-wide
- The confidential nature of the business entities constrains the collection of sensitive information
- The research analysis may not be timely enough. The dynamism of the economy means that the outlook of the economic phenomena may change from time to time
- Limitation of in-depth literature for the exchange controls. Not many cases can be studied for the research purpose, and

- The effects of exchange controls cannot be isolated from the economy as a whole. Therefore, the global economic downturn blurred the effects of the government's recovery plan.

5.6 Implications for Further Research

Further research can be carried out to determine the theoretical relationship of the controls and economic performance and how companies are limited in their financing methods during the imposition of the controls.

Since there are not many cases which are similar to the case in Malaysia, the efficiency of the controls are not reflected in full, even up to the point of completion of this research. The next research on this issue may have better in-sight and clearer results.

BIBLIOGRAPHY

1. **Alexander K. Swaboda.** (ed.), *Capital Movements and Their Control,* (Leiden: A.W. Sijithoff, 1976), p.180.
2. **Andreas S. Gerakis**. "Pakistan's Export Bonus Scheme". *Finance and Development,* vol.11 no.2 (June 1974), pp.10.
3. **Asian Development Bank**. *Critical Issues in Asian Development – Theories, Experiences, Policies,* Oxford University Press, 1996.
4. **Asian Development Bank.** "Emerging Asia – Changes and Challenges", Asian Development Bank, 1997.
5. **Athukorala, Prema-Chandra.** "Malaysia: The Macroeconomy", *In Modern Malaysia in the Global Economy: Political and Social Changes into the 21st Century,* edited by Colin Barlow. Aldershot: Edward Elgar, forthcoming.
6. **Baldwin.** Foreign Trade Regimes and Economic Development in The Philippines, supra note 12, pp.76-78.
7. **Bhagwati, Jagdish.** "The Capital Myth: The Difference between Trade in Widgets and Dollars", *Foreign Affairs* 77, no.3 (1998): 7-12.
8. **Bhanoji Rao.** (2001), *East Asian Economies – The Miracle, a crisis and the future* McGraw Hill.
9. **BIS** (Bank of International Settlement). International Banking and Financial Market Development. Basle: 1998.
10. **BNM** (Bank Negara Malaysia). *Annual Report of the Board of Directors for the Year Ended 31 December 1997,* Kuala Lumpur: BNM.
11. **BNM** (Bank Negara Malaysia). *Annual Report of the Board of Directors for the Year Ended 31 December 1998,* Kuala Lumpur: BNM.
12. **BNM** (Bank Negara Malaysia). *Annual Report of the Board of Directors for the Year Ended 31 December 1999,* Kuala Lumpur: BNM.
13. **BNM** (Bank Negara Malaysia). *Annual Report of the Board of Directors for the Year Ended 31 December 2000,* Kuala Lumpur: BNM.
14. **BNM** (Bank Negara Malaysia). *Annual Report of the Board of Directors for the Year Ended 31 December 2001,* Kuala Lumpur: BNM.
15. ***Business Times*** 2001, London, 11 April.
16. **Calvo, Guillermo A**. "Varieties of Capital-Market Crises", Center for International Economics Working paper no.15. College Park: University of Maryland, 1995.

17. **Chin Kok Fay** with **K.S. Jomo**. (2001), "Financial Intermediation and Restraint", In Jomo K.S. and Shyamala Nagaraj (eds) *Globalisation versus development: Heterodox perspectives.* MacMillen, Basingstoke.

18. **Chowdhury, Anis** and **Islam, Inayatul.** (1993), *The newly industrialising economies of East Asia.* Routledge, London.

19. **D.Shirreff.** "Can anyone tame the currency market?" *Euromoney*, September 1993, p.66.

20. **Daniels, J.** and **D. VanHoose.** 1999, 'International Monetary & Finance Economics'. International Thomson Publishing.

21. **Dornbusch Rudiger.** "A Thai-Mexico Primer: Lessons for Outmaneuvering a Financial meltdown". *The International Economy* (September/October 1997): 20-23, 55.

22. **Dornbusch, Rudiger, Iian Goldfajn** and **Rodrigo O. Valdes.** "Currency Crises and Collapses". *Brookings Papers on Economic Activity 2* (1995): 219-93.

23. **European Economy**: *Annual Report* 1993.

24. ***Financial Times***. "Asia in Crisis" (5 Part Series), 12-16 January 1998.

25. **Fisher, Stanley.** "Lessons from a crisis". *The Economist*, 3 October 1998, pp.19-23

26. **FPB** (Foreign Policy Bulletin). "SE Asia Currency Focus of IMF/World Bank Annual Meeting" (Experts from Statements by Malaysian Prime Minister Mahathir Mohamad, George Soros and Michel Camdessus). *FPB* 8, no.6 (1997): 24-33.

27. **Garnault, Ross.** 1998, "Exchange Rates in the East Asian Crisis". *Southeast Asia's Economic Crisis.* ISEAS.

28. **Gerald Tan.** "The Asian Currency Crisis". Times Academic Press. (2000) pp.51-190, 255-266.

29. **Goldfajn, Iian** and **Rodrigo O. Valdes.** "Aftermath of appreciation". *IMF Working paper 5650.* Cambridge, Mass: National Bureau of Economic Research, July 1996.

30. **Goldfajn, Iian** and **Rodrigo O. Valdes.** "Are Currency Crisis Predictable?" *IMF Working Paper 97/159.* Washington, D.C.: IMF, Research Department, 1997.

31. **Gomez, Edmund T.** and **K.S. Jomo.** *Malaysia's Political Economy: Politics, Patronage and Profits.* Cambridge: Cambridge University Press 1997.

32. **Hale, David.** "Rubin's Folly?" *The International Economy* (September/October 1997): 14-19.

33. **Henderson, Callum.** *Asia Falling: Making Sense of the Asian Currency Crisis and its Aftermath.* Singapore: McGraw-Hill, 1998.

34. **Hiebert, Murray.** "Big isn't Beautiful". *Far Eastern Economic Review*, 5 March 1998, pp.44-46.

35. **Hill, Hal.** "Malaysian Roulette". *Asian Wall Street Journal*, 9-10-October 1998.

36. **Holloway, Nigel.** "All Together Now: Needed Banking Standards for a Volatile Region". *Far Eastern Economic Review*, 22 May 1997, pp.83-84.

37. **Hussain, Mumtaz** and **Steven C. Radelet.** (1999), "Exports and Asia's Recovery". In the *Asia competitiveness report.* Geneva: World Economic Forum.

38. **IMF.** *Annual Report on Exchange Arrangements and Exchange Restrictions 1983*: pp.66 (Argentina), 144 (Brazil), 146-147 (Colombia) and 372 (Paraguay).

39. **J. Williamson** and **M. Miller.** "Targets and Indicators: A blueprint for the co-ordination of economic policy", *Policy Analyses in International Economics* No. 22, IIE, 1987.

40. **Jomo K.S.** (1998), "Malaysia's debacle: Whose fault?" *Cambridge Journal of Economics*, 22(6): 707-722.

41. **Jomo K.S.** (2001), *Malaysia Eclipse – Capital Controls.* Zed books Ltd.

42. **Jomo K.S.** and **Natasha Hamilton-Hant.** (2001), *Malaysia Eclipse-Financial regulation, crisis and policy response.* Zed books Ltd.

43. **Kenichi Ohmae.** April 1999, *The Borderless World: Power and Strategy in the Interlinked Economy.* Revised edition. Harper Collins publisher.

44. **Kristof, N.D.** 1998, "Global Economy Needs Revamp". *The Straits Times*, 24 September, p.41.

45. **Krueger.** Foreign Trade Regimes and Economic Development Turkey, supra note 12 pp.188-90.

46. **Krugman, Paul.** "Saving Asia: It's Time to Get Radical". *Fortune*, September 1998, pp.7-14.

47. **Krugman, Paul.** (1994), "The Myth of Asia's Miracle" *Foreign Affairs.* 73 (Nov): 62-78.

48. **Kuttner, R.** 1998, "Causalities of free market worship". *The Straits Times*, 10 September, p.37.

49. **Kwan C.H.** 1998, "Coping With Capital Flows In East Asia" – *Coping With Capital Flows in Asian Countries.* Nomura Research Institute. ISEAS.

50. **Lim, Linda.** (1999), "Capital controls – a drag on Malaysian Recovery. *The Straits Times*, 19 June.

51. **Little, I.M.D, T. Scitovsky** and **M. Scott.** 1970, *Industry and Trade in Some Developing Countries: A Comparative Study.* Paris: OECD.

52. **Maanen, J.V.** 1983, "The Fact of Fiction in Organisational Ethnography" in J.V. Maanen (ed) Qualitative Methodology – An Updated Reprint of the December 1979 Issue of *Administrative Science Quarterly.* California: Sage Publication.

53. **Malaysian Institute of Economic Research** 2001, 16th National Economic Briefing, "Malaysian Economic Outlook 2001-2002". 2nd Quarter 2001 update.

54. **Marsick, V.J.** (1990), "Altering the Paradigm for Theory Building and Research in Human Resource Development". *Human Resource Development Quarterly.*

55. **Maxfield, Sylvia.** (1998), "Capital flows and financial crisis – effects of international portfolio flows on government policy choice". Manchester.

56. **Mead, W.R**. 1998, "Markets are biggest threat to peace". *The Straits Times*, 29 August, pp.46.

57. **Ministry of Finance** 1998, Government of Malaysia. Economic Report.

58. **Ministry of Finance** 1999, Government of Malaysia. Economic Report.

59. **Ministry of Finance** 2000, Government of Malaysia. Economic Report.

60. **Ministry of Finance** 2001, Government of Malaysia. Economic Report.

61. **Montes, Manuel F.** (1996), "Country responses to massive capital flows". United Nations University/ World Institute for Development Economics Research Working paper No. 121, Helsinki, September.

62. **National Economic Action Committee Report** 1998, Malaysia.

63. **Nurul Islam.** Foreign Trade and Economic Controls in Development. The Case of United Pakistan (New Haven: Yale University Press 1981) pp.121-36.

64. **OECD.** Controls on International Capital Movements: The Experience with Controls on International Financial Credits, Loans and Credits. (Paris 1982).

65. **Ong Hong Cheong.** (1996), "Exchange rate fluctuations and macroeconomic managemnent, 1980-1995". Paper presented at PEO specialists Meeting, Osaka, 27-28 Sept.

66. **Ong Hong Cheong.** (1998), "Capital flows in East Asia – coping with capital flows and the role of monetary policy: The Malaysian Experience, 1990-95". *NRI* 1998.

67. **Ong Hong Cheong.** (1999), "Restoring East Asia's Dynamism-Exports and economic recovery: A Malaysian Perspective". *NRI* 1999.

68. **Park Yong Chul.** (1994), "Concepts and issues", in H.T. Patrich and Y.C. Park (eds). *The financial development of Japan, Korea and Taiwan: Growth, repression and liberalisation.* Oxford University Press, New York.

69. **Parke, A.** 1993, "Messy research, Methodology Pre-dispositions and Theory Development in International Joint Ventures", *Academy of Management Review* 18(2) pp.227-268.

70. **Perry, C.** and **Zuker-Sherritt, O.** (1992), "Action Research in Graduate Management Research Programs". *High Education*, vol. 23, March, pp. 195-208.

71. **Perry, C.** (1995), "A Five Chapter Ph.D. Thesis". Research Workshop Handout. Southern Cross University, Australia.

72. **Porter, Michael.** (1990), "The Competitive Advantage of Nations". New York: Free Press.

73. **Radelet, Steve** and **Jeffrey Sachs.** "Asia's Reemergence". *Foreign Affairs* 76, no.6 (1997): 44-59.

74. **Rasiah, Rajah.** (1994), "Capital industrialisation in ASEAN economies". *Journal of contemporary Asia*, 24(2): 197-216.

75. **Rasiah, Rajah.** (2001), "Malaysia Eclipse – Pre-crisis economic weaknesses and vulnerabilities". Zed Books Ltd.

76. **Rodney H. Mills, Jr.** "The Regulation of Short-Term Capital Movements in Major Industrial Countries" in; and Sachs, Jeffrey D, Aaron Tornell and Andres Velasco. "Financial Crises in Emerging Markets: The Lessons from 1995". *Brookings Papers on Economic Activity*, no.1 (1996): 147-215.

77. **Sachs, Jeffery D.** 1998, "Global capitalism: Working it out, making it work". *The Straits Times*, 17 September, pp.40-41.

78. **Sachs, Jeffery D., Aaron Tornell** and **Andres Velasco.** 1996, "Financial Crises in Emerging Markets: The lessons from 1995". *Brooking Papers on Economic Activity*, no.1: 147-215.

79. **Samuel Bassey Okposin** and **Cheng Ming Yu.** (2000), "Economic Crises in Malaysia, Causes, Implications & Policy Prescription" Chapter 7. pp.113-124.

80. **Shirreff. D.** 1993, "Can anyone tame the currency market?" *Euromoney*, September, p.66.

81. **Sloman, J.** "Economics", Second edition, 1994.

82. **Stiglitz, Joseph.** (1998), "The role of international financial institutions on the current global economy". Address to the Chicago Council on Foreign Relations, Chicago, 27 Feb. [*http:/ www.worldbank.org/html.extme/jssp 022798.htm*].

83. **Stiglitz, Joseph.** (1999), "What have we learned from the current crises: implication for banking regulation" Remarks at the conference on 'Global financial crises: Implication for banking and regulation', Federal reserves Bank of Chicago, Chicago, IL, 6 May 6.

84. **Swidrowski.,** Exchange and Trade Controls, supra note 10, pp.70-84.

85. ***The Economist*** magazine, "Of take-offs and tempests" 14 March 1998, p.92.

86. ***The Star*** newspaper, 2 May 2001.

87. **Uma Sekaran.** "Research Methods For Business". 3rd edition.

88. **Verbit.** supra note 11. pp.176-81.

89. **W John R Woodley**. "Multiple currency practices", "Finance and Development", vol.3 no.2.

90. **World Bank.** 1998, "The East Asia: The Road to Recovery", World Bank, Washington D.C.

91. **Yin, R.K.** 1989, "Case Study Research- Design and Methods'. *Applied Social Research Methods Series* vol.5. Newbury Park: Sage.

92. **Zikmund.** "Research Methodology". 1999, Dryden.

INDEX